Emerging Technologies

Emerging Technologies

Blockchain of Intelligent Things to Boost Revenues

Errol S. van Engelen

BEP BUSINESS EXPERT PRESS

Emerging Technologies: Blockchain of Intelligent Things to Boost Revenues

Copyright © Business Expert Press, LLC, 2020.

Cover image licensed by Ingram Image, StockPhotoSecrets.com

Cover and interior design by Exeter Premedia Services Private Ltd., Chennai, India

First published in 2020 by
Business Expert Press, LLC
222 East 46th Street, New York, NY 10017
www.businessexpertpress.com

ISBN-13: 978-1-95253-810-0 (paperback)
ISBN-13: 978-1-95253-811-7 (e-book)

Business Expert Press Big Data, Business Analytics, and Smart Technology Collection

Collection ISSN: 2333-6749 (print)
Collection ISSN: 2333-6757 (electronic)

First edition: 2020

10 9 8 7 6 5 4 3 2 1

Printed in the United States of America.

Abstract

This book is targeted to help a broad audience such as students, professionals, and business and technology managers to learn about the possibilities created by the convergence of blockchain, Internet of Things (IoT), and artificial intelligence (AI). The book takes you from the convergence of blockchain and IoT, via the most important Blockchain of Things projects like IOTA and the industries which are heavily being disrupted, into the *Blockchain of Intelligent Things*, which essentially adds the business value of data science and AI. Further topics you will find in this book include *required skills, jobs and future, Industrial IoT (IIoT) platforms*, and *opportunities, challenges, and trends* of the *Blockchain of Intelligent Things*.

Keywords

digital transformation; emerging technologies; blockchain; Internet of Things; IoT; data science; artificial intelligence; AI; blockchain of things; blockchain of Intelligent Things

Contents

Preface

For everyone in business and technology, interested in blockchain, Internet of Things (IoT), and artificial intelligence (AI).

The convergence of blockchain and IoT powered by data and AI is on the agenda of several big companies and some of them have already started using its implementations, initiatives, and solutions in various projects.

Audience

This book is for anyone interested in and responsible for vision, projects, and implementations of blockchain, IoT, and AI in medium-sized companies and large enterprises. This would include business and technology managers, IT professionals, and last but not least, business or technology students, looking to broadening their knowledge and expertise.

What This Book Covers

This book is specialized in blockchain, IoT, and AI and the convergence between each of these technologies. Obviously blockchain can enhance AI-powered IoT systems. The following chapters help you to get a better understanding.

Chapter 1, *Blockchain of Things*, introduces you to the convergence of blockchain and IoT. You will learn what the benefits and challenges are, why the blockchain is the security of IoT networks, and why your productivity will boost when applying Blockchain of Things.

Chapter 2, *Applications and Projects*, helps you to discover the most important Blockchain of Things projects running at this moment, including IOTA, PowerLedger, VeChain, and WaltonChain.

Chapter 3, *Industries and Verticals Being Disrupted*, helps you to find industries in which the Blockchain of Things is going to play a big role.

Per industry I've given examples and use cases to inspire the reader. You will surely find your own industry or vertical there too.

Chapter 4, *Blockchain of Intelligent Things*, provides you with the added business value of data science and AI. This added value is displayed in various industries and verticals such as automotive, energy, human resources, and marketing.

Chapter 5, *Required Skills, Jobs, and Future*, provides you with the information about blockchain, IoT, and AI salaries in the United States. Other topics include the skills gap, recruitment, and future scenarios of work, skills, and education.

Chapter 6, *Industrial IoT (IIoT) Platforms*, gives you an overview of the most important business platforms for Blockchain of Things projects. It also shows which service provider owns the platform.

Chapter 7, *Opportunities, Challenges, and Trends*, helps you to discover how you can use AI, blockchain, and IoT to find more business opportunities. Other topics include business threats such as security, cyber war, and cyber threats and how to use AI to combat them. It also gives you an overview of the future of Blockchain of Intelligent Things.

All chapters include a 'chapter takeaway' and 'management questions for your business' paragraph.

To Get the Most Out of This Book

It helps if you have some familiarity with blockchain, IoT, and AI. Also, if you are a business professional or manager with an interest in these technologies, or a technology professional or manager with an interest in business, this book is right for you too. Readers may be looking for a methodology to engage in blockchain, IoT, and/or AI projects. I would like to refer those readers to my previous book *New World Technologies: 2020 and Beyond*, ISBN 9781948976879 (for the eBook) and 9781948976879 (for the paperback). This book gives readers an overview of the most important emerging technologies and also contains a methodology for engaging in digital transformation and emerging technologies projects. So please get this book if you're looking for a methodology.

Reviews

Please leave a review. Once you've read and used this book, why not leave a review on the site that you purchased it from? Potential readers can then see and use your unbiased opinion to make purchase decisions. Thank you very much!

Acknowledgments

I want to thank everyone who helped in the creation of my book. In technology projects, many in the role of client, employer, or colleague helped me directly or indirectly to obtain the proper image of the impact technology has on business. I would also thank the many online experts and content publishers who increased my knowledge of blockchain, Internet of Things, and artificial intelligence.

I hope you enjoy reading while improving your business and technology skills and knowledge with *Emerging Technologies: Blockchain of Intelligent Things to Boost Revenues.*

Errol S. van Engelen
Rotterdam, April 2020

CHAPTER 1

Blockchain of Things

With the history of cybercrime, Internet of Things (IoT) systems are not safe today. Hackers could attack different components—the physical device, the network, the encryption, or the software. It means that the obvious issues of privacy, security, and identity verification must be addressed.

This further implies that a basic IoT system for businesses will have to include plenty of different integral components—a safe platform, edge tiers managing the devices, contextual rules, multiple protocols, various data formats, and storage. Of course, all these elements will have to be interoperable between unique and dynamic networks.

Our current IT systems seem to be simply underqualified for such large tasks. They often fail to provide required security, leading to dangerous situations of exposing users' data to unauthorized parties. Blockchain technology might not be a magic bullet with all the solutions to the challenges IoT is facing, but it sure can help solve a few of the major problems. As IoT applications are distributed in nature, it is reasonable to apply a distributed ledger technology (DLT) which blockchain provides.

Blockchain technology answers the issues of trust, privacy, single point of failure, scalability, record keeping, timestamping, and consistent reliability. Together with IoT, it could build a healthy system which allows devices to register and validate themselves on the network, while business activities could execute automatically through smart contracts. Figure 1.1 is a graphic of the merge between blockchain and IoT.

There would be no worry about attacks like denial of service or identity theft because there will be no single point of failure in such a system.

To illustrate the benefits of a blockchain-based IoT system, imagine a business setting with complex trade routes and logistics such as delivery service, for example. Distributed ledgers would be employed to track and record everything that is happening to each item or package. This will

Figure 1.1 Blockchain of Things

Source: Bloctonite

provide transparency of the origin of items and packages, their current delivery status, and so on.

The possibilities of applying these two technologies together are limitless. Take another example: insurance. The main use case of blockchain in insurance would be smart contracts and the enhancing of several other elements such as processing claims.

Although success may seem miles away, IoT is coming, and DLTs such as blockchain are going to be at the center of it. If you own a business, it is time you start exploring ways of benefiting from IoT or you'll be left behind.

What Is Blockchain?

At its simplest, a blockchain allows parties to cocreate a permanent, unchangeable, and transparent record of exchange and processing, without having to rely on a central authority. Where previous generations of digital technology have been about *data* and *information* and how to exchange it faster and more securely, blockchain is about the *exchange of value* and how to make it instant and decentralized.

Within this context, many see blockchain as part of the process of digitalization that has been underway since the 1960s. But while blockchain is undoubtedly part of this process, it is also a dramatic departure from it. Previous technologies were about carrying out the same business processes faster and more efficiently. Blockchain is about completely redefining how business processes are implemented, and even how they are designed in the first place.

How Does Blockchain Work?

In all blockchain transactions, there are four fundamental components:

A consensus protocol: It manages *how* transactions are recorded and agreed between members. It removes the need to centralize information, say through a siloed database, to prove the validity of a transaction.

This is probably the biggest breakthrough associated with blockchain, the way it allows parties who don't trust one another to reach an agreement. It also prevents the problem of "double spend" which, until bitcoin, had been the biggest problem for digital currencies. The double spend problem is when a digital coin or token can be spent more than once because it can be duplicated in a similar way to cutting and pasting in a Word document. Consensus protocols can also prevent fraudulent transactions from being wrongly validated.

A ledger: It is what many people are referring to when they discuss blockchain. This is a public record of all transactions stored across a distributed peer-to-peer network of servers. Once a transaction is verified, it is added to the ledger as a "block."

Rewards or incentives: A blockchain solution requires *either a reward system,* such as "miners" earning bitcoin or Ether, or *an incentive mechanism* to ensure that competing interests are aligned.

Within bitcoin and Ethereum, mining is the process of adding transactions performed during a certain time period on to the ledger and is the means by which nodes on the network reach a secure, tamper-resistant consensus. Miners confirm the transactions within blocks through completing complex mathematical problems in order to be able to write them into the ledger. They are paid (or rewarded) in bitcoin. All of the miners compete to be the first to solve the mathematical problem that allows them to write the transactions to the ledger. In bitcoin, this is called "proof of work."

The number of bitcoins miners receive is reducing over time, dependent on how much is left in the network. In total, only 21,000,000 bitcoins will ever exist. Mining therefore provides two functions: first to release new bitcoins into the network as miners are paid and second to provide motivation for people to provide security for the system.

Even in situations where there's no need to give people a financial reward for mining, there is a strong need for *economic incentives*, for example, finding good reasons for participants in an industry to share data together on the blockchain. The rewards-versus-incentives argument is one of the main ways to differentiate how the economics of a blockchain solution will work.

Smart contracts: These are pieces of code that allow applications to be developed on the blockchain. They are secure because, on a blockchain, there is no one single point of failure; the code exists on every node in the network. This means that there is no one place that the code can be manipulated without all the others on the network noticing.

Why Are Companies Shifting Toward Blockchain?

Smart Contracts

The primary reason for such a growth in blockchain technology is because it is simple and easy. Let me explain this in depth taking the example of the transaction system. The conventional transactional model is great for a simple transaction. What if you want to shift focus on legislating the long-term behavior of assets transparently? Then the current system is not very efficient. Blockchain has the provision of smart contracts which if used properly can become a great way to transact and release payment. These are preprogrammed contracts set on certain conditions. These conditions determine how an articular transaction unfolds. Smart contracts find application in different fields; from business transactions to real estate, companies are exploring different ways in which they can use smart contracts.

Trustworthy System

One of the key features of blockchain is that it makes the entire monetary transaction a simple and easy process. With the help of this technology, companies can reduce costs and offer an opportunity for business growth and intrastate maintained at a lower cost which otherwise is not possible with the conventional system that we are using. Moreover, blockchain processes transaction faster since it is not a centralized system. The unalterable feature of blockchain offers its users an unprecedented level of trust in the system. Also, it allows the user to raise a query on the transaction in real time.

Digital Identity

Now, this is an important aspect of blockchain which companies like Microsoft and IBM are trying to explore. Today, there is a need for a system which can give us quick access to all the credentials and information about a person. This can not only be helpful for a single company rather, but also be beneficial for every sector like health care, education, and human resource. The decentralized system will offer easy access to all the information in the system from anywhere. This will not only save time but also ensure that the data is real and unalterable.

What Is the IoT?

The first person to mention the "Internet of Things" was Kevin Ashton, the cofounder of the Auto-ID Center at MIT. This is how he defined the IoT:

> If we had computers that knew everything there was to know about things—using data they gathered without any help from us—we would be able to track and count everything, and greatly reduce waste, loss and cost. We would know when things needed replacing, repairing or recalling, and whether they were fresh or past their best.

Put simply, the IoT encompasses everything that is connected to the Internet. This includes everything from smartphones, smart thermostats, smart TVs, smart watches, headphones, gaming console, and almost anything else you can think of.

All of these are everyday objects that are connected to the Internet and recognized by other devices. As long as the device is able to contribute info to a database, it can be considered the IoT.

We have just scratched the surface of what the IoT is; however, you may still be wondering what the potential benefits of the IoT are. Why would we even want everything to be connected to the Internet?

Well, let's try to explain this in simple terms.

Benefits of the IoT

One of the important reasons for designing the IoT is to make our every-day lives more convenient. When a device is connected to the internet, it has the ability to send or receive data, or even do both. This capability makes things smart, and of course, for good reasons.

Earlier I mentioned some devices, so let's use smartphones again as an example. With your smartphone, coupled with a reliable Internet pro-vider, you can listen to any song or watch any video you want. This is possible, not because you have all of them stored on your phone but because they are stored somewhere else, and your smartphone can send data (requesting for that video/song) and then receive data (streaming that video/song on your smartphone).

Thus, being smart doesn't mean having a large storage space in your smartphone; rather, it means being able to connect to one. Isn't that great?

So when it comes to IoT, everything connected to the Internet can be divided into three categories:

1. *Anything that receives and sends information*: This refers to sensors such as carbon monoxide sensors, motion sensors, light sensors, and water-leak sensors. When connected to an IoT gateway, these sensors acquire data automatically from the environment with which we can make sound decisions.
2. *Anything that receives information and then acts on it*: For example, this is what happens when you make use of your TV remote. You send a command to change the channel or turn on or off and your TV responds. From a distance, you can tell a device what to do.
3. *Anything that can do both*: The IoT is capable of doing both (1) and (2), collect, send, and act on the information received.

All three have a great advantage, that of relying on each other without human intervention. That said, are there any drawbacks? Yes!

Of course, this new innovation has its downside and that has to do with security and privacy threats. Currently, most IoT devices are not secured as they are vulnerable to hack attacks. Back in 2018, millions of IoT devices were hacked. However, IoT manufacturers are now paying more attention to security and privacy as they warn users to take every precaution in securing their devices.

So what now? At the moment, the best thing you can do is to combine the blockchain with the IoT.

Benefits of Merging

In the last decade, several technologies emerged with the promise to revolutionize economy in general by disrupting almost every sector of the industry: AI, Big Data, IoT, and blockchain.

Research has identified several benefits of using blockchain for IoT: building trust, reducing risk with superior security, reducing costs, and acceleration of transaction.

Summarizing, we can say that benefits of IoT and blockchain convergence are twofold:

1. Blockchain can be a solution to important IoT challenges.
2. IoT and blockchain combined can provide benefits across several industries and in that way speed up the adoption of both technologies.

Blockchain as a Solution to IoT Challenges

Privacy

The use of encrypted, distributed, verifiable place to store and share data also means that data can be trusted by all parties involved in the supply chain. Only those with an authorized cryptographic public and private key can read the information, or with no human oversight, machines and smart devices will securely record transactions that take place between themselves.

Furthermore, once data is stored in the chain, it cannot be changed or modified in any way, which makes collected data absolutely accurate and precise. However, if records are originally recorded inaccurately, then blockchain will not fix this.

This also implies that hackers can't collect confidential or sensitive information by compromising IoT devices or manipulate the system in any other way.

Security

The security issue is identified in many research and surveys as the highest concern among potential adopters of IoT technology.

With an estimated 8.4 billion IoT devices and predicted by 2020 that the number could exceed 20 billion, plus the fact that IoT devices are astonishingly insecure in its current form, utilization of the blockchain becomes necessary.

Hackers have thus far managed to entirely disable cars remotely, control implanted cardiac devices, even use a refrigerator to attack businesses, and launch the world's largest DDoS attack.

With the most robust encryption standards, blockchain ensures a much needed layer of the security in the IoT stack. Any harmful, malignant, and dangerous entity/actor will have to bypass this superior layer in order to access IoT data or IoT devices, which will make cyber-attacks way more difficult and time consuming, if possible at all.

Blockchain and IoT Use Cases Across Several Industries

Besides security and privacy, smart contracts provided by the blockchain technology are also considered as the game-changer for IoT applications.

Basically, with the encoded logic, it's possible to create agreements which will be executed when certain conditions are met. This can be useful as the foundation for many use cases and different scenarios.

Supply Chain

The biggest benefit of the IoT and blockchain convergence is expected in supply chain and logistic in several industries.

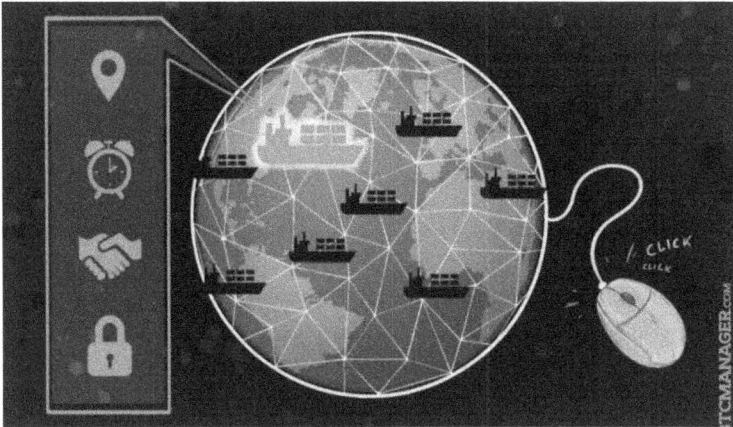

Figure 1.2 Maersk and IBM

Source: BTC Manager

IBM, Maersk, and 40 other organizations are trying to improve and speed up a very complex and time-consuming process of international trade and shipping and bring transparency to its unavoidable bureaucracy. Figure 1.2 is a graphic of this cooperation between IBM and Maersk.

Blockchain technology with IoT and sensor data ranging from temperature control to container weight enable shippers, shipping lines, freight forwarders, port and terminal operators, inland transportation, and customs authorities to interact more efficiently through real-time access to shipping data and shipping documents in a single shared view of a transaction without compromising details, privacy, or confidentiality.

Using blockchain, smart contracts allow all these parties involved in international trade to collaborate in cross-organizational business processes and information exchanges, all backed by a secure, reputable audit trail.

IBM has launched another supply chain initiative that harnesses the combination of IoT and blockchain.

Together with Walmart, they are trying to address longstanding problems around food safety and traceability since nearly 28 million people fall ill in the United States every year as a result of foodborne illnesses.

To efficiently address those issues, and at the same time prevent massive losses for retailers and suppliers during a recall, IBM and Walmart developed a solution to track products in near real time through its supply chain, from the farm to the consumer.

All participants, from growers, suppliers, processors, distributors, retailers, regulators, to consumers, have access to secure, reliable, and traceable information regarding the origin and state of food for their transactions.

Each node on the blockchain could represent an entity that has handled the food on the way to the store, making it much easier and faster to see if one of the affected farms sold infected supply to a particular location with much greater precision.

Before moving the process to the blockchain, it typically took approximately seven days to trace the source of food. With the blockchain, it's been reduced to 2.2 seconds! That significantly reduces the possibility that infected food will reach the consumer.

Logistics

Pharma and many other industries are considering solutions that can generate value leveraging on IoT and blockchain in a relevant way.

In the context of strict regulations, whereby proof is needed that shipped medicines have not been exposed to specific conditions that might compromise their quality (mainly on the level of temperature), the IoT sensor data is verified against predetermined conditions in a smart contract in the blockchain, to offer this proof.

The contract validates that the conditions meet all of the requirements set out by the sender, their clients, or a regulator and triggers various actions, such as notifications to sender and receiver, payment, or release of goods.

Solving Counterfeit Goods Problem

According to the International Chamber of Commerce, the negative impacts of counterfeiting and piracy are projected to drain U.S. $4.2 trillion from the global economy.

Counterfeit goods are everywhere—fashion and retail products, digital gadgets and media, software—but the most severe implications are in the pharmaceutical market where counterfeit drugs are now responsible for around 1 million deaths per year.

Tracking drugs on the blockchain throughout their lifecycle—from manufacturer to end consumer—could facilitate counterfeit drug identification or assist drug recall management.

Blockchain's smart contract functionality with a digital signature along with the use of IoT devices could deliver an effective, real-time tracking as the drug moves through the supply chain, with complete transparency and verifiable proof of what has been delivered to who and by whom.

Insurance

The combination of blockchain and the IoT is shifting ahead of the simple telematics model to the connection of real-time IoT data in several intelligent automated insurance policy applications.

Thus claims management, fraud management, health insurance, and property and casualty insurance will be improved in many ways with smart contracts combined with IoT data from wearable personal technologies, sensors on objects (vehicles, shipping containers), and location-based sensors (factories, warehouses, homes, alarms, cameras, industrial control systems).

For insurers that have relied on agents and brokers, the ability to directly access objective, unfiltered granular and precise customer data will represent an enormous change.

Peer-to-Peer Energy Trading and Facility Optimization

Building facility management and energy management is one of the areas where IoT technology already proves its value.

Brooklyn Microgrid is one of the interesting projects where the convergence of blockchain and IoT improves energy efficiency and facility optimization through peer-to-peer marketplace for distributed energy, in this case, coming from local solar micro grid.

Neighbors in Brooklyn are buying and selling solar power from each other, but more than enabling small-scale trading of environmentally friendly electricity, this project will have battery storage units within the grid in order to ensure supply during the next storm-related emergency.

Smart meters, except measuring energy production and consumption, communicate with each other and form blockchain where these transactions are taking place.

The potential of blockchain and IoT in the energy industry could be transformative, and over the past two years, we have seen a host of start-ups with similar peer-to-peer marketplaces for distributed energy, trying to disrupt global energy market, still trapped in a previous era.

Blockchain as a Security Tool

Issues IoT Currently Faces

Since it was first conceptualized in the 1980s, IoT has come a long way to the bleeding edge technology we are standing at today where there is even an Internet of self-driving cars. The number of IoT devices projected to be a part of the average household is expected to jump from around 10 to near 500 by 2022. IoT connectivity is a given when purchasing tech products before customers can even demand it; the product design now leans toward interconnectivity despite the current IoT snafus.

What are the main issues IoT currently faces that hinder its effectiveness and even put consumer data in danger?

Let's keep in mind while reading this section that most emerging IoT platforms are cloud-based and have a central hub that then provides back-end services to smart devices. This setup makes it so that the devices are what are receiving data, while on the other end the centralized hub is the service provider.

Here are the most significant problems with centralized IoT:

- *Security:* This issue is brought up time and time again when it comes to IoT. With so many connected devices it makes it difficult for users to secure their personal data and use patterns. The more devices that are connected the more vulnerabilities and security threats. It also creates more gateways for companies to suffer hacks.
- *Cloud attacks:* As stated in the intro to this section, most IoT has cloud architecture. This means that large, and often

sensitive, amounts of data will be stored on the cloud. This makes cloud providers easy targets for hackers. Where there is centrally consolidated data in an obvious location there are looming cyber-security threats.

- *Expensive:* Not only is IoT currently expensive to manage and deploy efficiently, the World Economic Forum has estimated that if one cloud provider was hacked it could cost $50 billion to $120 billion dollars in damages. Integration is expensive and it is likely that the cost of devices with IoT capabilities will also rise.

- *Privacy and data storage:* Companies will be responsible for massive amount of consumer data that they can either sell or leave in insecure centralized repositories. Being able to harness that data, store, and adequately protect it is an insurmountable challenge, and hoarding it in the cloud has proven to be an incredibly risky strategy. Centralized IoT ramps up the Personal Identity Information (PII) sprawl crisis that consumers fall victim to daily.

- *Consumer skepticism:* Adoption for centralized IoT has been slow and it is clear that all involved parties have valid concerns about moving forward. Regardless, IoT is a runaway train as manufacturers continue to create IoT devices. Consumers are skeptical that IoT service providers will protect them and also don't necessarily trust the IoT devices themselves and their ability to store and transmit data securely.

- *Inadequate infrastructure:* There are major connectivity issues with IoT and the client–server model that facilitates connection. While it does work presently, it lacks long-term scalability. Looking at the numbers predicted for 2022 for how many IoT devices will need network support, it is hard to imagine a functioning network supported by current, already inefficient and insecure centralized models.

- *Blockchain issues with scalability:* The blockchain scalability problem is regarding the limits on the amount of transactions that can be done under the bitcoin network. This blockchain network has limitations as the blocks in the bitcoin blockchain are of a certain size and frequency and thus can't process a flood of transactions at once. With the blockchain technology being integrated into various mainstream sectors, we will surely be seeing more blockchain advancements in the future and lower down the number of blockchain limitations.

How IoT Can Benefit From Blockchain

Centralized services might be working for now, but they are not a sufficient long-term IoT solution to support device design of the future on a massive scale. Moving data and backend services away from centralized servers will be the key to IoT capabilities reaching their full potential in a secure way. In Figure 1.3 you can see how blockchain security supports IoT.

Decentralized IoT will make device connectivity and data storage trustless—*meaning* nobody needs to trust anybody else in order for the system to function—through nodes that can operate without a centralized authority. A distributed model is more efficient, secure, affordable,

Figure 1.3 Blockchain security for IoT

Source: Computeworld

and will unlock even unforeseen residual benefits for IoT that have yet to be predicted.

Here is a list of the top benefits of decentralizing IoT:

- *Improved security:* Blockchain offers devices unparalleled security infrastructure that blows cloud-based storage out of the water. Distributed networks lack a single point of entry or vulnerability for hackers to enter. Cryptographic signatures make hacking incredibly difficult; any messages originating from anywhere other than the authentic origin will be null and void on the network.

- *Tamper-proof data:* Decentralized applications carry a much lower risk of falling victim to tampering and fraudulent activity. Why? Because DLT uses asymmetrical cryptography to timestamp and immutably store transaction data and other related information on the ledger.

- *More affordable:* When security vulnerabilities are removed through placing IoT on distributed networks and storing data via DLT and blockchains, IoT becomes more affordable. Service providers currently have a monopoly on IoT and the cost of supporting devices. Decentralization will make IoT more accessible, and damage costs from hacks can be more easily prevented or avoided all together. Intermediaries that operate centralized IoT systems and all associated costs will also be eliminated through decentralizing IoT.

- *Trustless (or unsure):* Trust between all parties and devices using IoT will use the distributed ledger to verify and use smart contracts to automate. Trust will never be placed in a centralized service provider or other actors to store data or be in control of their device connectivity. DLT can automate services through code to act as the intermediary for data flow.

- *Autonomy:* Blockchains enable smart devices to act independently and self-monitor. These mini "Distributed Autonomous Corporations" could be comprised of a decentralized IoT that is able to operate on its own according to the predetermined logic of a specific household or industry. This could completely remove intermediary players and central authority to have completely automated financial services or insurance settlement distribution, for example.

Automating Trust

How much does trust cost your company? The OECD estimates that U.S. $461 billion worth of counterfeit goods are sold annually. That's 2.5 percent of global trade. In other words, 1 out of 40 items on the global marketplace is a fake. If you're heading a company, one of your responsibilities is to make sure that none of those fake items ends up as a part in your products or, even worse, in the market with your company's name on it. Prevention typically requires big spending on duplicative testing, manual auditing, reconciliation, legal fees, insurance, and more.

In the airline industry, for example, many carriers hold planes on the ground longer and keep more spare parts on hand than technically necessary, as well as skip potential savings available from used parts and planes—all because they can't fully trust their provenance. Trust also comes at a cost in the health care industry, where physician networks and hospitals need to confirm each new clinician's credentials: educational history, licenses, regulatory history, and more. That typically takes months, during which the clinician can't work, and requires contacting more than a dozen entities. Health care payers spend more than $2 billion a year maintaining provider databases.

Fortunately, emerging and established technologies can now be combined to provide companies with ways to automate trust in physical, digital, and human assets. It's a premise centered on blockchain, which is then integrated with one or other essential eight technologies, such as IoT and artificial intelligence (AI). And once trust is automatic, it's not just costs that fall. Whole new business opportunities emerge.

A More Transparent Supply Chain

A supply chain is a bit like a relay race. Your component or product travels vast distances, with frequent hand-offs from one participant to another. But with automated trust, you can keep track of these assets in real time,

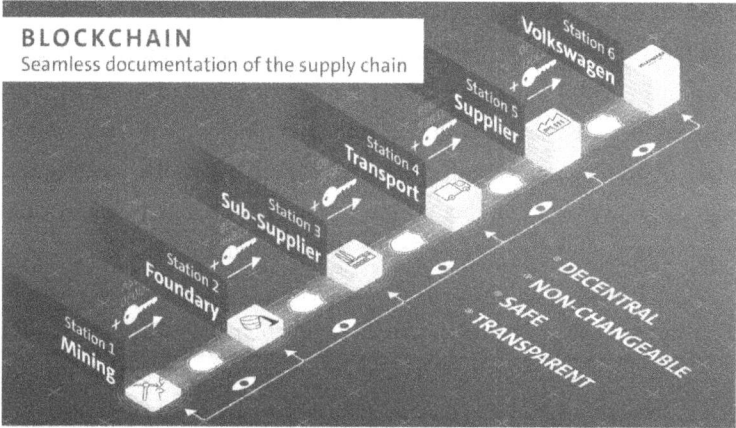

BLOCKCHAIN
Seamless documentation of the supply chain

Station 6
Volkswagen

Station 5
Supplier

Station 4
Transport

Station 3
Sub-Supplier

Station 2
Foundary

Station 1
Mining

*DECENTRAL
*NON-CHANGEABLE
*SAFE
*TRANSPARENT

Figure 1.4 Transparent supply chain

Source: Volkswagen newsroom

both while they're racing through a complex supply chain and as they change hands among partners, vendors, and customers. A transparent supply chain can be seen in Figure 1.4.

The need for trust starts when a product or component leaves the factory or farm. A manufacturer that has implemented automated trust creates a digital "birth certificate" with specifications, provenance, cost, and other relevant data. It then enters this birth certificate (usually an IoT tag) into its existing ERP system, integrated with blockchain to create a secure, immutable, cryptographically sealed record. This record is instantly available, in identical form, on the different servers of the participants in this supply chain, such as the manufacturer, logistics providers, distributors, and wholesalers.

Next come IoT sensors, to record location, temperature, ambient vibrations, and other measures to provide continuous end-to-end provenance. The logistics provider scans the sensors to connect them to the blockchain and to the digital birth certificate. As assets change location and condition, IoT sensors gather the data. Blockchain stores it, securely and immutably, with a timestamp on the servers of all of the participants.

Permission to transfer custody, such as from the logistics provider to the warehouse, takes place on the blockchain, which once again creates an immutable, decentralized record. Smart contracts—digitally signed agreements that software executes and enforces—on the blockchain can automate these transfers. Before the warehouse accepts delivery, for example, a smart contract can check the IoT-derived data to make sure that temperature and vibrations during transport were within the permitted range. If problems occurred, the smart contract consults the record to assign responsibility. Another smart contract can automatically calculate (and in some blockchains, even issue) the payment due.

With trusted data, participants can layer on AI-powered analytics. Algorithms can flag parts for maintenance, further analysis, or even immediate interdiction if necessary. AI can also mine data for further insights, such as forecasting maintenance or determining more efficient use.

If a company wants to keep track of digital assets, the same process applies: The maker of the software or service creates a digital birth certificate and enters it into the blockchain. The blockchain then records use, alteration, and sales, all with an unchangeable, distributed record, with smart contracts to automate the workflow, and with AI to draw meaning from the data.

Verification Made Simple

Whether you're dealing with sensitive data, machines, or health care decisions, it's important that only the right people with the right qualifications have access. Utilities, for example, may need to confirm hundreds of contractors in a hurry when they hire extra crews to respond to a natural disaster. If a technician without the right credentials so much as touches a pipe, the company typically has to pay a big fine—and redo the work. Yet it can currently take a full day to confirm a single contractor, possibly adding unneeded delays and cost to repairs.

Here, too, a system powered by blockchain, IoT, and AI can be the solution. In this system, long before the natural disaster took place, contractors' employees have enrolled in the blockchain with their biometrics. They have entered their personal information, credentials, and qualifications. The organizations that issued these credentials have confirmed the employee's claims, through a workflow tool, also on the blockchain.

Now, when a utility company hires these contractors, IoT sensors, using AI-powered facial recognition, verify the individuals' identity and offer the utility a confirmed record of their qualifications. The block-chain records each of these verifications, creating a work history. Add on another layer of AI to analyze these employees' records, and the company can get fast insights into which employees should do which task, in which place, at which time.

Any industry in which the workforce needs verified qualifications could benefit. If a given individual's profile is available on this system, the hiring company can get detailed, trusted information on work history and qualifications—just as if they were already in-house employees. As the gig economy grows, the need for independent contractors to show trusted credentials will grow too.

Building a New Business

Automated trust doesn't just offer secure, real-time insights into supply chains, employees, and operations. With the right rules of engagement, all users can have their own unique digital signatures with varying levels of permission attached. The owner of the data can grant some users the right to see it, others the right to alter it, and others no access at all. These varying levels of permission make sharing data both flexible and safe.

With trusted data and the ability to share it selectively and securely, new revenue streams and efficiencies are created:

- *Decentralized, customized pricing.* Parent companies can use blockchain, combined with AI and the IoT, to gather, share, and analyze data to enable more effective pricing decisions at the point of sale.
- *Trusted data-driven business models.* Whether it's developing new products or marketing existing ones, automated trust in transaction data—which can inform AI models to forecast markets and consumer tastes—makes new businesses feasible.
- *Collaborative R&D.* It's a common problem in joint R&D ventures, in sectors as diverse as pharmaceuticals and gaming: Who owns how much of the result? Combining blockchain and AI can track and analyze who contributed what value to the intellectual property and product.

- *Consumer engagement.* When you can securely share selected data, you can better share quality and sustainability practices. Consumers, for example, can confirm the provenance, production methods, and validity of perishable food.
- *Decentralized identities.* With blockchain and AI powering and confirming consumer profiles, consumers can select which aspects of their identity to share with whom. Firms authorized to access these profiles can offer (with the help of AI) customized, enhanced services and experiences based on consumer trust.

With trusted information (from IoT), secure ways to record and share it (through blockchain), and analytics to draw out insights (from AI), the opportunities are endless. That's why automating trust isn't just a way to cut down on counterfeit goods, unqualified personnel, and all the costs of confirming assets and people. With the right approach, it's a foundation for rapid growth in the digital economy.

The Next Productivity Revolution

When a system fails on the factory floor, each second of downtime equals dollars down the drain—about $22,000 per minute for some automobile manufacturers.

With those stakes, advances in smart factory technology that enable efficiency, advanced machine-to-machine connectivity, and high-speed communication—down to the microsecond—can't come fast enough. Efficiency leads to productivity increase as shown by Figure 1.5.

Imagine:

- A beverage factory that uses the same assembly line to fill bottles with different drinks
- An auto manufacturer with a modular production cell that can build different types of cars on the same line with near-zero downtime
- Alerts that tell technicians about potential part and system failures before they happen

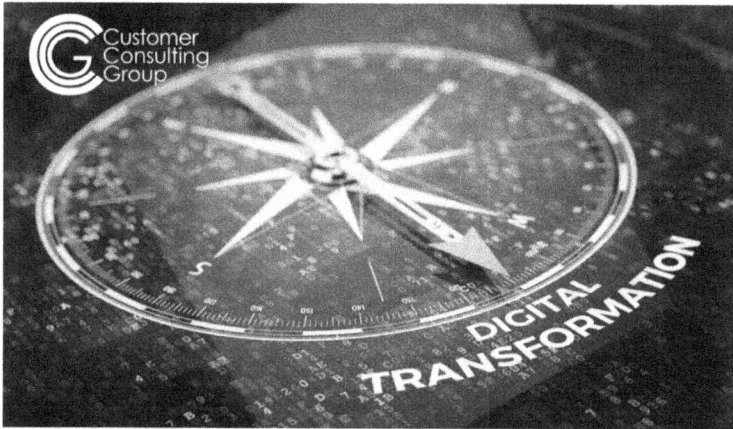

Figure 1.5 Increase productivity

Source: Customer Consulting Group

- Machines that can sense objects and avoid collisions work collaboratively with humans

The factory of the future will be highly efficient and highly connected. Some of the latest innovations drastically improve communication while addressing increasing bandwidth requirements.

Here are three trends adding intelligence to Industry 4.0:

1. *Advanced industrial communication enables predictive maintenance.*
   If the smart factory has a calling card, it's the level to which it has pushed machine-to-machine connectivity and communication, enabling a host of other capabilities.

   While gigabit Ethernet time-sensitive networks (TSN) increase connectivity and the speed of data pinging between manufacturing devices, emerging technologies can harness that data from the factory floor and decipher it in real time. Industrial Internet of Things (IIoT)-related applications allow technicians to anticipate part and system failures before they happen and improve subsequent generations of product development.

2. Machine vision and human–machine interaction increase quality.
Cobots—or collaborative robots designed to work alongside humans—represent one of the fastest-growing market segments in robotics, projected to reach nearly $9 billion by 2025.

These sophisticated machines can detect the proximity, speed and location of people or objects in defined zones through TI mmWave radar, giving robotic arms 'vision' to safely help workers load machines or pick components out of bins, for example. Machine vision can also enable greater product quality by testing tolerance, dimensions and other material attributes.

3. Edge analytics promotes efficiency.
On the factory floor, some critical movements can't wait for machine learning in the cloud. Instead, they demand insights and decisions closer to action, such as a robotic arm that needs to maneuver around workers to do its job. Edge analytics puts intelligence and decision-making capability right into the robot arm.

Most modern factories are already benefiting from smart technology and IIoT to some degree. In the factory of the future, smart technology will add flexibility and modularity to even the most efficient single production line.

Chapter Takeaways

- Introduction to the blockchain and the IoT.
- IoT and blockchain combined can provide benefits across several industries, and in that way speed up the adoption of both technologies.
- Blockchain and IoT use cases across several industries.
- The most significant problems with centralized IoT and the top benefits of decentralizing IoT.
- IoT and blockchain combined are seen as automated trust which improves your reputation.
- Adding intelligence to the IoT and blockchain combined will lead to the next productivity revolution.

Management Questions for Your Business

- What are the main requirements for implementing and running an IoT platform?
- What technologies are best suited to solve risks associated with a centralized IoT platform?
- What technologies are best suited to add intelligence to the IoT platform?
- What are total forecasted costs or budgets and forecasted results or savings?
- What are business cases with a positive cash flow?

References and Additional Reading

Kim, S., and D.S. Deka. 2019. *Advanced Applications of Blockchain Technology.* Springer Nature, Singapore.

Laurence, T. 2017. *Blockchain for Dummies.* John Wiley & Sons, Hoboken, NJ.

Tapscott, A., and D. Tapscott. 2016. *Blockchain Revolution: How the Technology Behind Bitcoin is Changing Money, Business and the World.* New York, NY: Penguin Random House.

www.e2e.ti.com/blogs_/b/thinkinnovate/

www.medium.com

www.openforum.com.au

www.strategy-business.com

www.ventsmagazine.com

www.weforum.org

CHAPTER 2

Applications and Projects

Blockchain is currently being explored for use in IoT projects. Blockchain can be used for security applications in IoT projects. By merging blockchain with IoT, the data collected by smart devices in the IoT network can be securely stored. Data is the most valuable component of an IoT network and securing it using blockchain can be vital in improving the IoT network. A few IoT applications and examples are shown in Figure 2.1.

A few ways in which blockchain can be used with IoT are as follows:

- Smart contracts can be implemented within the IoT network. Smart contracts are contracts which get executed automatically when certain predefined conditions are satisfied. The involved parties can be certain that each entity involved in the contract will work as decided without the need of an intermediary.
- The smart machines connected in the IoT network can record data and transactions among themselves without human intervention. This will result in accurate and tamper-proof records.
- Traditional IoT uses centralized storage and processing systems, but with blockchain and its decentralized, distributed, and secure network, the data will be safe and easily accessible.

Some possible applications of Blockchain of Things are as follows:

- *Pharmaceutical industry*: In some countries, pharmaceutical companies are required by law to maintain certain medicines at prescribed temperatures at all times during transport and

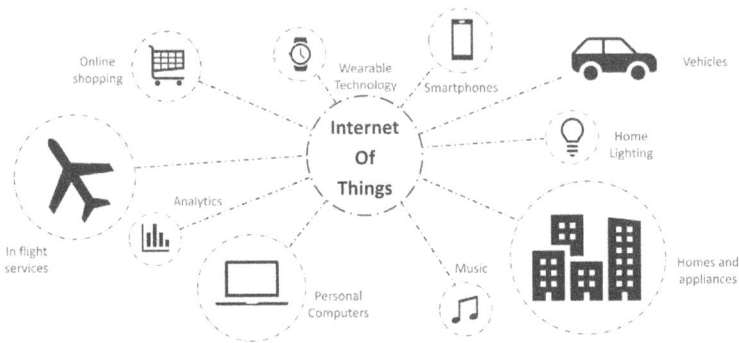

Figure 2.1 IoT applications and examples

Source: Edureka

distribution. IoT technology using blockchain smart contracts can help to maintain the data as proof of compliance.

- *Self-driven taxi industry*: When blockchain is used with self-driven taxis, it will fully automate the taxi industry. This will eliminate the safety issues currently faced by drivers and passengers despite steps taken by taxi companies. The taxi can accept a booking and even payment from the customer using blockchain. This will also result in savings for both the business and customers.
- *Smart energy*: As the energy generation becomes decentralized and consumers start using alternatives like solar energy to power their homes, blockchain can be used to buy and sell excess energy generated by consumers among themselves.
- *Supply chain*: Products like Modum use Blockchain of Things to automate the supply chain. Any kind of product can be easily tracked at all stages of the supply chain. Consumers can be sure of where the product came from, which is more relevant in the food business. This will also help consumers be sure the product is not fake.

The use of Blockchain of Things is still in its nascent stage. There will be technical and economic challenges to overcome for successful implementation of blockchain in IoT. Blockchain technologies may need to be customized to fit better for use with IoT technologies. This would be the next technological advancement in IoT.

Top Blockchain of Things Projects

If you search for Blockchain of Things projects, you can easily see that there are plenty of them that are looking for ways to improve the world around us. Following are some of the larger Blockchain of Things projects.

Ambrosus

Overview

Ambrosus is building a blockchain-based ecosystem for supply chains, ensuring the origin, quality, compliance, and proper handling of items tracked by the network. Ambrosus' scope of business involves improving supply chains for essential products, specifically food and medicine, and high-value products. Ambrosus seeks to redefine supply chain management while utilizing blockchain technology and IoT systems.

What Problem Does Ambrosus Solve?

The complexity of supply chains today can potentially lead to forged or falsified information. The time it takes to identify and locate where and when along the supply chain the issues arose can cost a company large sums of money in lawsuits for selling bad or harmful products. Besides the aspect of falsified, distorted information, global supply chains involve plenty of paperwork while products or materials pass from one company to another, including manufacturers, warehouses, distributors, and retailers.

Implementation of blockchain technology into this process can also cut expenses significantly and make the distribution process much simpler and more effective. Once the information about goods is automatically recorded and stored on the blockchain, it becomes accessible by everyone. Thus, every participant of the logistics chain, including the end customer, can check reliable info about products by simply accessing the records.

Product and Vision

The Ambrosus team found out in the early days that the Ethereum network was too limited in its ability to handle all of the data the Ambrosus network required, so they created a protocol that runs above it. By creating a secondary blockchain coupled with a distributed storage system and smart contracts, Ambrosus becomes scalable to any degree their own system can handle all while being verified again on the Ethereum blockchain.

Why blockchain? The decentralized nature of blockchain is the most tamper-proof solution to counterfeits, and furthermore tracking the flow of goods from hundreds of suppliers, producers, distributors, retailers, and customers becomes extremely complicated and confusing. Smart contracts help to streamline the entire process and make it clean and simple. The added value of immutability and traceability throughout a supply chain is beneficial to any supply chain system. Information is key to success in the manufacturing process and is likely why the supply chain industry and supply chain management is a growing industry right now.

A few use cases for Ambrosus are listed as follows:

- *Food origins and tracing*: Suppliers and distributors sign off the batches of products by linking their individual identity to the signatures. This allows precise attribution of responsibility for quality assurance and prevents fraud.
- *Logistic sustainable improvement*: Combination of temperature sensor and surroundings sensors to assess any container's unusual physical parameter variation and bad exposure. Measurements at the container level are performed and alarms are triggered, informing the logistics directly.
- *Food delivery without the middleman*: Food orders with partner restaurants and cafes would be placed through the decentralized marketplace and customers would pay directly to the delivery people without the payment passing through the middleman.

Tokenomics: What Is the AMB Token?

The native token of Ambrosus is called Amber (AMB), which is used to help trace products through their value chain, linking the information gathered to the records and keeping the database up to date. Amber tokens are sent to the network alongside readings and remain locked in the Measurements Smart Contract until a batch has completed its movement through the supply chain. Amber is also the fuel for the Ambrosus ecosystem, used to access the network services, interact with the sensor systems, and enter commercial agreements assured by smart contracts. As Amber is used to perform different actions within the Ambrosus ecosystem, the more usage the Ambrosus platform has, the higher the demand for AMB should be, therefore, adoption is the key to grow.

Growth Potential and Roadmap

Supply chain solutions are becoming one of the first areas of mass adoption for blockchain technology. Among other blockchain platforms that offer solutions for supply chain management Ambrosus is the one that, to a great extent, focuses on quality assurance of products, specifically food and medicine. This assurance is guaranteed via sensors, attached to the product during its life cycle, which represents another USP. The core value proposition of Ambrosus is to be a sensor agnostic platform. It provides data repositories and management systems that enable as many sensors as possible to talk to the blockchain. Ambrosus has a unique distinction from other blockchain companies targeting the food supply industry: they have the backing of several major organizations, including the United Nations and multiple government institutions in Switzerland.

Ambrosus Team is doing a great job communicating with investors through blog updates and Twitter interaction.

IOTA

"Internet of Things Application," more commonly known as IOTA, is a cryptocurrency that has been making some waves across the markets. Since its release in mid-2016 it has received plenty of attention, with its

Figure 2.2 Blockchain and IoT project IOTA

Source: CryptoNewsZ

creators calling it "the missing puzzle piece" required to kick start the so-called "Machine Learning Economy," an economy which will focus on allowing devices to trade anything from storage, computation/analytics, to electricity and sensor data. In Figure 2.2 the IOTA logo is shown.

It's similar to other cryptocurrencies in the sense that it's a publicly distributed ledger, but the similarities pretty much end there. While Bitcoin and most available coins utilize the so-called blockchain architecture, IOTA can't be categorized as a blockchain project since it's based on a completely novel invention called "The Tangle." The Tangle is a new data structure which doesn't depend on blocks, chains, and miners. Instead it employs a decentralized, blockless, peer-to-peer architecture called "Directed Acrylic Graph" (DAG). DAG architecture requires that each network participant who wants to make a transaction actively participate in the consensus of the network by approving two previously made transactions.

This means that potential transactors "earn" the right to transact in IOTA with zero fees by attesting on the validity of past transactions, thus ensuring that the entire network remains stable and functional.

Overall, 354 unique entities have shown interest in IOTA, including 68 official partnerships/collaborators, 135 entities working with the foundation on joint projects, 77 IOTA Data Marketplace participants, and 56 entities that built one or more IOTA-based proof-of-concepts and 49 references to academic publications about IOTA. We'll be taking a closer look at some of IOTA's standout collaborators, determining what exactly each of them brings to the table.

The most important collaborations include the following:

- *Volkswagen*: Driverless technology is one popular potential application of IOTA's data marketplace. Sensory data used to drive these autonomous vehicles can be introduced into the IOTA database and then used to improve the quality of future products. This is why Volkswagen, one of the world's biggest car manufacturers, decided to team up with IOTA and explore what they called the "Digital Car Pass." This technology is set to be released sometime in 2019 and will look to reliably capture data from Volkswagen vehicles as well as allow Volkswagen owners to easily purchase software and services like parking or highway tolls.

- *Mobility Open Blockchain Initiative (MOBI):* In line with IOTA's dedication to "improving driving safety and affordability, supporting autonomous and electric vehicle development and infrastructure, fostering ride and car-sharing applications, and connecting mobility participants in a new peer-to-peer ecosystem," the project joined the MOBI to further those goals. The collaboration was confirmed in 2018 and will see IOTA work with companies like BMW, Bosch, Ford, General Motors, Groupe Renault, ZF, Blockchain at Berkeley, Hyperledger, Fetch.ai, IBM, and Aioi Nissay Dowa Insurance Services USA to foster an ecosystem where businesses and consumers have security and sovereignty over their driving data, manage ride-share and car-share transactions, and store vehicle identity and usage information

- *Fujitsu*: Fujitsu is a well-known tech company and an IT service provider/product maker that has also taken an interest in IOTA and its protocols. Fujitsu sees IOTA as the basis for "Industry 4.0" and expects it to become a key element of future manufacturing and supply chains. Building trust and integrity in these areas is very important and IOTA can help with that by providing a Tangle-based cryptographic ID system designed to track product components and the overall production status.

- *Microsoft*: Much noise was made about IOTA allegedly partnering up with Microsoft back in late 2017. Microsoft blockchain specialist Omkar Naik delighted the IOTA community when he confirmed his company's "excitement" that they are "partnering" up with the IOTA foundation and are proud to be associated with the data marketplace initiative. The quote led to IOTA including Microsoft as an official member of its data marketplace, which was apparently not the case. Microsoft representatives confirmed that their only official collaboration involves IOTA being a Microsoft Azure customer, with plans to deploy the mentioned data marketplace on the Azure architecture.

- *Other partnerships and implementations include*:
  - *Crypto Storage AG partnered with IOTA Foundation* to offer professional, multisignature storage solutions to holders of the MIOTA cryptocurrency. The announcement was made on January 9, 2019. The partnership mostly targets large private and institutional investors.
  - *eCl@ss* is looking to create an ecosystem of precise sensors which record data and categorize it through specific, unique IDs. With over 3,000 corporate entities on board, eCl@ss wants to deliver standardization and easy data transfers into the real world.
  - *Energinet, a Danish company,* signed a MoU (Memorandum of Understanding) with IOTA foundation in late January to explore implementations of IOTA in energy markets.
  - *IAMPASS* wants to provide high-availability data centers which will handle identity and access management services on top of IOTA's Tangle. Access control is a very important part of today's security management.
  - *Jaguar Land Rover* partners on a data collecting initiative. Jaguar wants to collect information on road conditions and vehicle performance and in return they offer IOTA tokens to their drivers. The partnership is a part of Jaguar's

initiative to tackle accidents, road congestion, and emissions in the automotive industry.

○ *Topocare* was one of the first grantees of the IOTA EDF (Ecosystem Development Fund) and has sought to implement a complex flood protection system. Topocare wants to leverage IOTA's Tangle to provide humanitarian improvements and catastrophe remediation or even prevention.

The list of entities that have collaborated with IOTA in one way or another is much more extensive. Only time will tell if IOTA will manage to push most of these partnerships past the typical "memorandum of understanding" or proof of concept type of deals and eventually create products that will be able to successfully operate on top of the Tangle.

Future Plans and Roadmap

The year 2019 has been a very exciting year for IOTA. They were able to make significant progress with their software offering, for example, with IRI, Trinity, individual client libraries, and Qubic. They also started new projects along the way. They have built a very capable Rust (a programming language) team working on the next generation of their node software that will transition through Coordicide. The goal of Coordicide is to reach consensus without the Coordinator, while ensuring scalability security and decentralization. IOTA with the Coordinator was scalable and secure, but not fully decentralized. The year 2020 is going to be even more exciting than last year, since IOTA has quite a few significant changes coming in the first half of 2020. The changes are improvements mainly based on collaborations with their research department, as well as building on some of the work that R&D has been doing for Coordicide.

OriginTrail

Overview

OriginTrail enables data sharing along supply chains. It helps companies exchange relevant data seamlessly, securely, and in a transparent way. Therefore it could become a new way for companies to build

Figure 2.3 Blockchain and IoT project origintrail

Source: OriginTrail.io

accountability, secure their brands, and increase efficiency. I've been looking into many supply chain projects, and OriginTrail is one of those that
has the potential to rival big companies in this field such as VeChain and
WaltonChain. OriginTrail aims to revolutionize supply chain management by building the first purpose-built protocol on the blockchain that
will allow supply chains to interact with each other even across international borders seamlessly. See Figure 2.3 to find OriginTrail's logo.

What Problem Does OriginTrail Solve?

It's becoming increasingly complicated to keep track between all points of
contact of modern supply chains. This is ultimately putting quality and
safety of products at risk. Global supply chains are becoming more and
more complex. OriginTrail outlines two main problems with the current
system:

- Fragmented data—collaboration between businesses can often
  be difficult.
- No suitable decentralized solution for supply chain data.

Every point along the production line relies on a chain of trust built out
of a principle called "one step back, one step forward." This means that
all companies involved need to trust each other until they can verify that

they received the quality they were promised. Therefore, proper auditing of merchandise and supply chains costs companies a lot of money and time. Put simply, with regard to current supply chains, there is no easy way to safely share information from one business to the next, due to the centralized nature of existing systems. A blockchain solution could not only create a more efficient and transparent log to keep track of shipments but also ensure trust along the supply chain as well as a way for customers to ensure they are buying high-quality products in the end.

Product and Vision

The blockchain that OriginTrail is utilizing is called the OriginTrail Decentralized Network (ODN). This is the network through which the supply chain data is shared. It is made up of several nodes located all around the world. Users and companies who wish to utilize the platform must run their own nodes, or they have to pay the owners of the nodes in Trace tokens. In return, the nodes will then encrypt, handle, and distribute their data. ODN is a protocol layer, so it can interact with any blockchain: Ethereum, IOTA, Hyperledger, and so on and a whole ecosystem of dapps can be built on top of it.

Interoperability is achieved by integrating globally recognized GS1 standards for Master Data. GS1 is a nonprofit organization that provides standard practices for the way in which companies communicate with each other. Additional data sets include IoT, GPS, and compliance data. OriginTrail is looking to integrate with existing systems like GS1 standard bar codes to provide more depth and reliability of tracking. This is necessary for adoption as it not only combines best practices and proven technology but also makes it easier for new companies to adopt Origin-Trail's technology.

Consensus among entities within the network and among the supply chain is achieved by performing cross-reference checks every time a new data set is added to the protocol. This ensures the entire supply chain is in sync regarding a particular batch of products and processes. Businesses and consumers can scan a code or enter information in an application interface and get back relevant information, such as where components were initially sourced from, who processed them, and more.

Tokenomics: What Is the TRAC Token?

The TRAC token is the means of compensation between supply chain data producers and data consumers on one side and the OriginTrail node holders on the other. By operating nodes and staking coins, investors will be able to earn additional tokens for their work in verifying transactions. TRAC provides the incentive to the nodes in the peer-to-peer network to perform the system functionalities. OriginTrail nodes are incentivized for performing:

- Discover and connect functionalities
- Supply chain consensus checks
- Data quality checks
- Data replication checks
- Data storage and management
- Filtering and delivering supply chain data

The total supply for TRAC is 500 million tokens, of which 285 million are currently in circulation. This is a great number, considering its application, in that it is not so large that it makes price growth difficult when the coin has total supply in circulation.

Growth Potential and Roadmap

OriginTrail is not the first company to recognize that supply chains could benefit a great deal from blockchain technology. Many competitors are fighting for a share in this potentially huge market. ShipChain, VeChain, WaltonChain, and Wabi are all involved with logistics and product authenticity in some way. All of these projects will be competing for clients and users.

OriginTrail has positioned itself to solve a significant industry problem and is making strides toward making its concept a wide-spread reality. Perhaps it would be better to find a smaller target market or industry to focus on in the beginning; it's great to have a wide range of industries utilizing your technology, but this strategy could also possess a thread in the future, especially in a crowded market where some competitors are already finding their niche.

VeChain

Overview

VeChain's primary purpose is to provide a blockchain-based platform which helps to improve the way the supply chain process is managed. VeChain aims to build supply chain blockchain technology for the real world by providing a comprehensive governance structure, a robust economic model, as well as advanced IoT integration. The platform offers retailers and consumers the possibility of determining the quality and authenticity of goods. At first glance, VeChain looks like it is just as a supply chain project, similar to WaltonChain, Wabi, or Ambrosus, but since their main net launch, people realize that VeChain is actually a blockchain platform. In February 2018, VeChain rebranded to VeChain Thor (VET). The rebrand moved the company beyond the supply chain into more general enterprise dapp solutions. The company was founded in 2015, with its ICO launched in August 2017. I feel VeChain is a project that every crypto investor should understand and be aware of, even if they choose not to invest in it.

What Problem Does VeChain Solve?

Counterfeit goods harm the prestige of a brand, reduce company profits, and influence consumer purchases. In fact, the total value of fake products globally is expected to reach $1.8 trillion by 2020 according to the 2018 Global Brand Counterfeiting Report. VeChain enables brands to monitor and manage their products along the whole supply chain, by placing radio-frequency identification (RFID) labels, QR Codes or NFC chipsets on them. In the case of RFID technology, these labels feature the entire history of a product, stored on a secure public ledger that can be viewed by buyers whenever they want.

The global supply chains of companies include many different stakeholders, operating in different parts of the world. Instead of stringing together a confusing mix of tracking software between stakeholders, companies can instead plug into the VeChain blockchain. This process doesn't just improve safety but will ultimately lead to an improvement in brand reputation and customer experience. Beyond counterfeit protection,

VeChain also enhances the efficiency of logistics systems through its simplified product tracking and by seamlessly connecting different parts of the supply chain. Global logistics is a complex topic and often includes several separate systems that vary across businesses. Because of this, tracking products in the supply chain can be a huge pain. This problem is solved though VeChain's blockchain technology. VeChain leadership has helped introduce this idea to many industries including tobacco and alcohol, frozen goods, automotive, luxury retail goods, pharmaceuticals, and cold storage.

Product and Vision

The following statement from VeChain summarizes their vision and function very well:

> VeChain's ambition is to develop a decentralized business ecosystem, which enables the flow of information securely and privately, building trust and transparency across borders and companies. VeChain leverages Blockchain to solve the problem of counterfeits and product traceability across supply chains and logistics namely in: Luxury Goods, Wines, Agriculture, Automobile, Transportation, Pharmaceuticals, Logistics and Audit Services.

We take a look at different aspects of the VeChain Platform.

Governance Model

The distribution of VET tokens not only determines consensus but drives the VeChain governance model as well. The stakeholders have the power to vote and elect the governing body of the VeChain Foundation, known as the Board of Steering Committee. This committee makes decisions on the technology, operations, and even public relations among other aspects.

Economic/Payment Model

VeChain's technology is aimed at corporations, which means the payment model has to be suitable for corporate needs and standards. As an enterprise, you want stable fees, but cryptocurrency price has too much volatility. VeChain solves this problem by utilizing a multilayer payment model. This feature helps enterprises to manage the payment of multiple dapps efficiently from one master account and also helps them to work better with business partners who do not want to deal with crypto assets.

Tokenomics: What Is the VET/VTHO Token?

As we have discussed before, VET economic model was designed to create more predictable and stable environments for retailers. Aside from VET, there will also be another crypto called VeChain Thor Token (VTHO). For holding VET, even if you aren't running a node, VeChain rewards you with THOR. This structure is similar to NEO's GAS and is used to run smart contracts and applications built on VET. This means that companies which rely on VeChain to track their supply chains and reinforce logistical flows have a real incentive to run their own node.

Growth Potential and Roadmap

In June 2018, the VeChain team reached a crucial milestone in launching the platform's main net. With the launch, the network moved off the Ethereum blockchain onto its own blockchain and, the team began swapping VEN for VET. The next step for the company is to expand the ecosystem with more dapps and strategic enterprise partnerships. The make or break of any blockchain project is their partnerships, especially for enterprise blockchain solutions. Talking about partnerships, VeChain has done a great job so far, when it comes to attracting big industry players as partners and clients. The most notable are PwC, DNV GL, BMW, and Kuehne & Nagel. VeChain is part of the PwC incubator program; DNV GL provides services to oil and gas, power, maritime, and renewable companies.

WaltonChain

Overview

WaltonChain is a decentralized platform which combines blockchain technology and the IoT using RFID technology to create a Value Internet of Things (VIoT). Although the technology of RFID is not new, WaltonChain has patented unique RFID chips that can read and write data directly to the blockchain, thus creating a genuine, trustworthy, and traceable business ecosystem, with complete data sharing and absolute information transparency. The name "Walton" from WaltonChain is a tribute to the original inventor of RFID technology, Charlie Walton. WaltonChain's logo can be found in Figure 2.4.

The RFID chip is developed by the subsidiary of WaltonChain, Silitec (technical support arm which specialized in manufacturing chips), and not outsourced. The chip costs under 5 cents per tag (industry average 15 to 20 cents) and will be lower in cost in the future due to economies of scale.

What Problem Does WaltonChain Solve?

The goal of WaltonChain is quite straightforward. While the public blockchain itself can be used on different types of use cases, the main

Figure 2.4 Blockchain and IoT project WaltonChain

Source: Incrypts

idea is to solve the problems in the supply chain management space. The project wants to coordinate data among large corporations by analyzing and tracking their products during every production and distribution step. The data is always saved on the blockchain to make sure it is tamper-proof and authentic. By utilizing the blockchain, third parties cannot easily "cheat" their data submission as everything needs to be confirmed and authorized by the blockchain.

The supply chain management industry has been facing a lot of problems in the past few decades. It is quite hard to track where the product originally comes from, as there are multiple third parties who get involved in the whole distribution process. The whole inefficiency problem becomes even worse when you involve import and export processes. And this is where blockchain can significantly improve such problem. By using RFID chips and utilizing the blockchain at the same time, every distribution step is tracked and must be verified by different entities.

Ecosystem

WaltonChain is made up of a parent chain, WaltonChain, and many other subchains (child chains), which run *independently* from the parent chain. The advantages of having child chains includes not congesting the parent chain, as the main transactions are run and stored in the child chains itself, instead of in the main chain like many other solutions. This offers unlimited scalability as having more child chains will not congest and overload the network of the parent chain.

The child chains are also *fully customizable* to the specific needs of the partners, such as being able to choose to become a public or private chain, having a different consensus algorithm from the parent chain, having hierarchical chains (child chains within child chains), hosting ICOs (Initial Coin Offerings) off these child chains, supporting different programming languages such as Solidity, C++, Java, Python, and so on. Companies are also able to directly purchase predesigned child chains that are already proven to work for other companies. The main aim of WaltonChain is to connect data. In the WaltonChain ecosystem, the multichain architecture formed by the parent chain and child chains follows the development trend of cross-industry coverage in the blockchain technology.

Use Cases

WTC-Food System:

WaltonChain teamed up with Fujian *Skynovo* IoT Technology to launch the world's first blockchain-based two-way traceability food authenticity platform, WTC-Food. WTC-Food will achieve mutual benefit for consumers, enterprises, and technology through the powerful and flexible data collection, information traceability, and credit endorsement. It will be widely promoted and applied in the food industry in the future. The food traceability system based on the WaltonChain blockchain technology and relevant hardware equipment includes video collecting equipment, sensors, smart terminals, a food traceability child chain, cross-chain nodes, and a data inspection system platform.

WTC-Garment System:

WTC-Garment, the world's first blockchain-based high-end clothing authenticity traceability platform, is developed by WaltonChain and China's leading high-end clothing brand, *Kaltendin*. The platform not only improves the efficiency of business operations of high-end clothing retailers in manufacturing, logistics, and store management through comprehensive smart solutions, but also provides an immersive shopping experience for customers. With the help of Big Data, the business can also analyze customers' needs and improve service quality, data utilization, store sales, and turnover rate.

Alibaba Cloud:

The partnership of ZhongChuan IoT (a subsidiary of WaltonChain) and Alibaba Cloud will provide Alibaba Cloud with multiple IoT application solutions designed by ZhongChuan IoT and help establish an AI hub for urban management and promote *smart city development*. The partnership also involves joining hands in the areas of *smart city solutions and blockchain application schemes.*

The partnership focuses on:

- *Promotion of WaltonChain blockchain technology* to achieve municipal and commercial IoT coverage
- *Establishment of new smart cities*
- *Construction of smart city schemes and their application:* resource allocation optimization and achievement of smart resource allocation through the blockchain and IoT technology

Future Plans

In 2020, WaltonChain will make some adjustments according to the market conditions. Marketing topics include release of full functionality of WTA (WaltonChain Autonomy) app for normal users and WTA staking in WTA app, WTC (Waltoncoin) buyback plan, and WTC token swap. Community topics include development of community autonomy, community voting, and establishment of WaltonChain Global Autonomous Foundation. Technology topics include child chain development, wallet upgrades, blockchain explorer optimization, implementation of traceability solutions, upgrading and promotion of WaltonChain Box, chip R&D, research of IoT-targeted hierarchy technology and construction of smart contracts.

Chapter Takeaways

- Introduction to the blockchain and the IoT.
- IoT and blockchain combined can provide benefits across several industries, and in that way speed up the adoption of both technologies.
- Blockchain and IoT use cases across several industries.
- The most significant problems with centralized IoT and the top benefits of decentralizing IoT.

- IoT and blockchain combined are seen as automated trust which improves your reputation.
- Adding intelligence to the IoT and blockchain combined will lead to the next productivity revolution.

Management Questions for Your Business

- What are the benefits and drawbacks of each block-chain-based platform described in this chapter?
- What are total forecasted costs or budgets and forecasted results or savings per platform?
- Which business cases have a positive cash flow?
- Which platform has the highest cash flow?

References and Additional Reading

Chowdhury, N., Dr. 2020. *Inside Blockchain, Bitcoin and Cryptocurrencies.* Boca Raton, FL: CRC Press.

Raj, K. 2019. *Foundations of Blockchain: The Pathway to Cryptocurrencies and Decentralized Blockchain Applications.* Birmingham, UK: Packt Publishing.

www.blockfyre.com

www.captainaltcoin.com/

www.chainbits.com

www.iotdunia.com

www.medium.com

www.waltonchain.tech

CHAPTER 3

Industries and Verticals Being Disrupted

Blockchain technology and cryptocurrency have reached an inflection point for enterprise adoption fueled by the combination of technological advancement and successful pilots for business use cases in financial services, global supply chains, government, health care, and many other industries. Enterprise adoption is still in the beginning phases but will ramp up quickly as innovators continue dreaming up more ways to use blockchain to disrupt and reinvent traditional business models. Industry leaders ahead of the curve on testing blockchain solutions have already experienced significant business benefits, including:

- *Better collaboration*: Current enterprise solutions involve localized ERP or other information systems. Localized data quickly becomes fragmented in complex global supply chains. Each link in the supply chain updates its own database on its own timetable. In contrast, blockchain provides an accurate, single instance of encrypted data that is always up-to-date and online, eliminating conflicting information created by data silos and system fragmentation.
- *Enhanced security*: The distributed, immutable blockchain technology offers inherent security advantages over traditional record-keeping systems. Every transaction must be agreed upon before it's recorded. Once recorded, every process, every agreement, every payment, and every task has a digital signature and record that can be validated and identified. The network itself is secured by a consensus mechanism for verification. This effectively makes it impossible for bad actors to launch attacks on networks at scale.

- *Faster traceability*: Any company with products that are a part of a complex supply chain understands how difficult it can be to trace an item back to its origin. Using the blockchain to record exchanges of goods creates an audit trail that offers instant visibility into the entire supply chain from origin to destination and every stop in between, reducing the need to rely on third parties to share information.

- *Greater transparency*: Each participant in the network receives a full copy of the blockchain (as opposed to maintaining individual copies), and they must all agree on the entire data history and each new transaction through consensus or mutual agreement. If anyone tries to change a previously accepted transaction, the network will immediately recognize the update as invalid and reject it. Thus, data on a blockchain is more accurate, reliable, and transparent than when the data is created through traditional processes.

- *Improved operations*: Any business function that relies on traditional processes is prone to human error and often requires validation. Blockchain technology offers widespread application across nearly every business function to add trust and transparency to any transaction. This facilitates transactions being completed much faster and more efficiently. Since the blockchain serves as a single digital ledger, the need to reconcile multiple ledgers among several parties is eliminated. Since everyone in the network has access to the same information, fewer intermediaries are needed to resolve disputes over conflicting data.

- *Reduced costs*: On top of cost reduction through automation, blockchain can also reduce the need for many third-party services. Because trust and transparency are inherent in every transaction, businesses can stop relying on third parties to settle trade disputes and instead trust the data on the blockchain. Businesses can also significantly reduce the scope of internal and external audits.

Blockchain together with IoT will most certainly disrupt quite a few industries and verticals, as you can see in Figure 3.1.

Figure 3.1 Industries disrupted by blockchain

Source: Blokt

Agriculture

The blockchain represents one of the technologies with the most prom-ise to provide more consistency in wide areas of the agricultural industry. Whether it is applied to managing warehouses, silos, and supply chains more intelligently, or utilized in the field as a tool to transmit real-time data about crops and livestock, there are few aspects of an agricultural operation that wouldn't benefit in one form or another from blockchain technology.

Examples and Use Cases

- *Community-supported agriculture (CSA)*: CSA operations bring together members of a community, who pledge to support a farming operation financially in return for fruits, vegetables, or whatever else a farm may produce. CSA farmers are likely to be younger, which means that they may be more inclined to new technologies.
- *Enhancing agricultural supply chains*: Producers, especially in the developing world, can also bolster their revenues by ensur-ing through blockchain technology that they are participants in a supply chain that targets a demographic willing to pay more for provenance and quality.

- *Modernizing farm management software*: As farmers integrate the likes of sensors, drones, and AI into their agricultural operations, they will see that a store of data kept on the blockchain allows them a greater level of prominence and differentiation among their competitors.
- *Overseeing farm inventory*: Utilizing a decentralized ledger on the blockchain that is easily accessible for all players in a given operation will provide more seamless communication regarding what needs to be done, whether that means harvesting crops, making storage-related adjustments, ordering new equipment, or otherwise.

Automotive and Connected Cars

On one hand, the automotive industry is the same it's always been: manufacturers selling their luxury pickup trucks and other models. On the other hand, the automotive industry is also showing signs of profound change. Vehicles are smarter than ever, with manufacturers embedding more sensors capable of everything from assessing postcrash injuries to tracking and disabling stolen vehicles. And we continue to move toward the age of autonomous vehicles. By 2025, approximately 8 million cars will be in transit while set to level 3 "conditional" automation or higher.

The blockchain has clear application for providing greater oversight and accountability in automotive supply chains and can also serve as a means by which drivers can view and understand how their vehicle's data is being shared and utilized.

Examples and Use Cases

- *Blockchain-based insurance platform*: As of 2015, there were 268 million registered vehicles cruising American roadways, and the need for insurance becomes abundantly clear when one examines how frequently those vehicles crash into objects, pedestrians, and other vehicles. In 2015, there were 32,166 deaths, 1,715,000 injuries, and 4,548,000 car crashes. The possibilities for blockchain-enabled vehicle insurance are many. Real-time policy updates, policy detail storage, and habit-based rate adjustment info could all be stored and automated.

- *Document and title transfer*: It's actually amazing how valuable a vehicle's title is. Not only can title thieves put your vehicles in their name, but just losing a title leads to the headache of acquiring a duplicate title. Without the title, it's virtually impossible to prove that a vehicle is actually yours. Blockchain platforms have already been conceived such that they store and verify information about the transfer of vehicle titles, as well as proof of sale, insurance, and other receipts that establish a clear record of ownership and legal documents.

- *Regulatory and environmental transparency*: Cars, trucks, and planes represent the greatest source of carbon dioxide emissions today. According to the American Lung Association, roughly 30,000 people die each year from health problems caused by the ingestion of vehicle-created pollutants. Drivers and brands using the potential of the IoT to track and report data related to emissions will become more environmental friendly. Using blockchain technology as an interoperable ledger for statistics could reduce the cost of implementing metrics.

- *Rewarding safe driving*: There's no denying the correlations between speed, recklessness, traffic accidents, and road deaths. At least one major car manufacturer has discovered a unique, blockchain-enabled way to incentivize safe driving. Information about a driver's habits is transmitted to the manufacturer's database, and that information is translated into a proprietary token. The thinking is that such a system could become even more effective if safe drivers could simply receive cryptocurrencies and/or lower their insurance premium. Figure 3.2 shows innovations in automotive to reward safe driving.

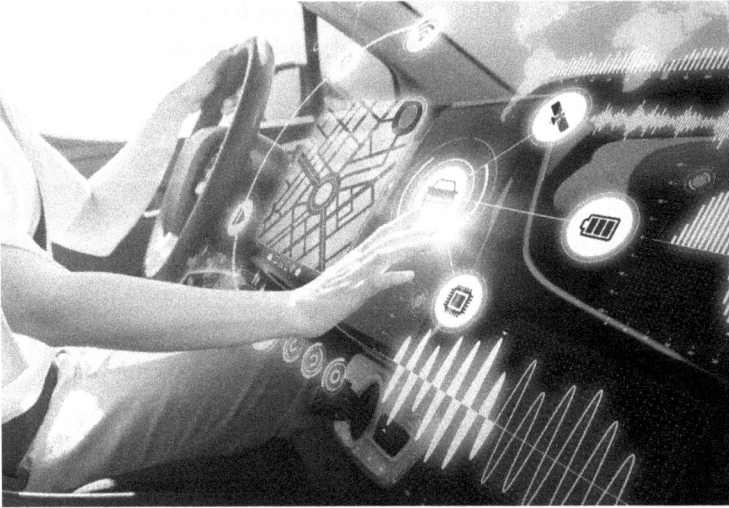

Figure 3.2 Innovations in automotive

Source: AutoFacets

- *Smart contracts for insurance*: Between 2005 and 2015, there was an average of 5,808,272 vehicle crashes per year in the United States. This amounts to 15,913 accidents per day. That means there're a lot of insurance exchanges, processed claims, and related investigations and transactions happening nearly all the time. The smart contract aspect of blockchain technology could also prove a valuable cost- and time-saver in adjusting rates, gaining consent from the parties involved in an accident.
- *Smart contracts for leasing/financing*: In Q2 2018, nearly 32 percent of new cars sold in the United States were leased. Many see leasing as a less daunting financial obligation than purchasing a vehicle outright. That's why leasing is gaining popularity. In 2015, Visa partnered with electronic signature company DocuSign to test blockchain-based smart contracts for leasing. These self-executing contracts simplify the process with fewer intermediaries.
- *Smart vehicle-derived data*: Smart vehicles generate an unprecedented amount of data that must be stored, shared, and sold.

A self-driving vehicle can generate as much as one gigabyte of data per second, and all of it will be put to use by somebody. It's possible that by 2020, car manufacturers will make a greater profit selling vehicle-derived data than from selling the vehicles themselves. That data must be secured, and the block-chain is an ideal candidate for use as a storage and transfer system for vehicle-derived data.

- *Theft prevention*: Stealing vehicles has never been so easy. According to *The Telegraph*, 9 out of 10 car thieves in England aren't caught, and keyless technologies have only made the problem worse. Blockchain has the power to provide next-level authentication, and it's not implausible to project that identity-specific benefit being tailored to vehicle security.

Banking and Financial Services

The impact of blockchain technology on the banking paradigm is already apparent and has been reflected in Figure 3.3. Data released by the World Bank indicates that more than 1.7 billion individuals around the world

Figure 3.3 IoT impacting financial services

Source: Finance Monthly

currently lack access to basic banking or financial services. Further studies conducted by the World Bank demonstrate that blockchain technology holds dramatic potential for promoting financial inclusion to the unbanked and underbanked. Traditional banks are highly aware of the potential blockchain technology holds to disrupt the financial industry. Major international banks, such as JPMorgan, Goldman Sachs, and Bank of America, have already heavily invested in the blockchain industry.

Examples and Use Cases

- *Crypto banking*: Financial institutions have taken note of cryptocurrencies. As the public understands how cryptocurrencies can diversify assets, high-value clients may urge banks to dive further into the crypto sphere. Banks who comply with regulators to pair their strong reputations with cryptocurrency offerings could have significant competitive advantage.
- *Interbank transactions*: Real-time interbank fund verification would unify banks and reduce fees. That would mean quicker wire transfers at a lower cost. Cash flow oversight is a task fit for automation, and the blockchain is a suitable candidate for the job.
- *Know your customer (KYC)*: Financial institutions face astronomical KYC requirements. KYC costs were $150 million in 2017 for institutions with $10 billion or more in revenue. Analysts expect the upward trend in KYC expenses to continue, at least until automation takes hold. The blockchain could be the anchor for automation in KYC practices.
- *Record sharing and storage*: Estimates show that between 60 and 70 percent of retail banks' records management costs can be eliminated by going paperless. This would cut operating expenses for processing divisions by as much as 25 percent.
- *Smart contract enforcement*: Smart contracts hold parties to an agreement, enforcing that contract with a self-executing algorithm. Money stays in escrow only to be released when the conditions of the agreement are fulfilled. Smart contracts substantially reduce the element of trust. This minimizes the risk of a financial agreement and the odds of ending up in court.

Charity

The annual income of the charity sector amounts to over $410 billion, but not all organizations active within the charity industry are altruistic. Data collected by the U.K. Fraud Costs Measurement Committee indicates that fraudulent charities capture more than $30 billion annually. Blockchain technology is able to deliver complete transparency in the distribution of assets donated to charity, allowing anybody to track the finances of any given charity and ensure that charitable organizations are held accountable for the fair and honest distribution of capital.

Blockchain technology not only offers charities a more efficient and open method of managing capital but also presents new opportunities for donors to provide charities with funds. Outside of direct donations, the blockchain industry also provides charities with new methods of capturing donations from donors.

Examples and Use Cases

- *Lower administrative costs*: While many see overhead costs as necessary, exorbitant administrative expense percentages are a red flag. The charities with the highest administrative costs actually spend more than they pass along. Blockchain-based platforms are aiming to provide charities with a marketplace to reach a ready-to-give audience, and these platforms take far fewer fees than traditional marketing and fundraising agencies. This platform can also provide proof of need and proof of receipt to ensure that the cause is indeed a worthwhile one.
- *Facilitating emergency aid*: There is no shortage of emergency aid-related scandals and snafus. More than eight years after relief for Haiti was completely bungled, the search for $500 million in missing donations continues. So, yes, the administering of emergency aid could use a complete blockchain overhaul. Emergencies are when most charitable donations are made, and being able to trace those funds' route to their destination is absolutely essential to avoid the waste and fraud that has become synonymous with emergency relief.

- *Giving chain transparency*: Lack of transparency degrades trust in charities and can come back to bite in several ways, deserved or not. For one, donors are unlikely to give to charities implicated in wasteful or illegal practices, decreasing whatever good they are doing. Additionally, well-meaning charities can be wrapped up in scandal—say, giving to suffering groups in a country where terrorism is rife—and can face undue sanctions as a result. The ability to trace funds from their point of donation to the recipient will necessarily crack down on wasteful spending, exposing fraudulent actors and reestablishing trust for donors who rightfully expect their money to be passed along under true pretenses.

- *Goal-driven fundraising models*: Sites like Kickstarter, GoFundMe, and Indiegogo have laid a successful blueprint for goal-driven philanthropy, with GoFundMe having reached a point where donations exceed $1 billion over a 12-month span. A blockchain-tailored philanthropic platform would imitate the goal-based fundraising model while relying on the technology to reduce fees for a less revenue-dependent system. Smart contracts are a particularly useful facet of the blockchain for this purpose.

- *Mining for charity*: Networks of high-powered computers hold such massive amounts of computer power that some are testing how spare computing power could be used to mine cryptocurrencies as a charitable venture. Thus far, these ventures have proven promising, with PC gamers successfully mining Ethereum to donate to Syrian children affected by violence. If more individuals can be convinced to put their spare computing assets to use as a passive form of charitable donation, it could prove a novel way to assist those in need.

- *Cross-border donation*: While 2009 saw a higher foreign donation total than 2016, figures tend to fluctuate by year, but are always substantial. For corporations supporting non-U.S. entities and other specific donors, these foreign donations can present some significant tax issues, and even result in asset freezes and financial penalties. The distributed nature of

blockchain-based transactions means that they aren't technically tied to any geographic region, which reduces associated
legal and taxation risks associated with cross-border philan-
thropic donations. Though regulation could emerge, several
entities are working to implement more efficient, cost-effective
cross-border giving with less red tape and fewer intermediaries.

Energy

Blockchain and energy tech are two of the most hyped technology movements in the world. The possibilities for the intersection of blockchain,
energy, and sustainable technologies are staggering, and there's plenty of
financial opportunity to back innovation. Energy management is projected to skyrocket to over $70 billion in value by 2022, according to
Zion Market Research. The entire sector is currently driven by rising
energy prices and increased regulatory pressure to reduce greenhouse gas
emissions toward more efficient innovation. New energy breakthroughs
will disrupt the sector, as shown in Figure 3.4.

Examples and Use Cases

- *Accelerating adoption of electric cars*: Bloomberg expects the
  number of electric cars to rise to 11 million by 2025 and 30

Figure 3.4 Technology breakthroughs in energy

Source: IndustryWired

million by 2030. Using blockchain technology, systems for monitoring peak energy prices could be maintained—and these systems could help charging station owners conduct transactions, make informed decisions about when and where to charge, and decide how much they can ask of those using their charging station.

- *Micro grids*: Centralized power grids are known for inefficiency and massive energy losses. Micro grids are aimed at remedying these losses. The distributed ledger technology that the blockchain utilizes could serve as the logical digital building block for users of these micro grids to monitor consumption and execute energy transactions.

- *Tokenizing energy*: Tokenizing renewable energy allows wind, solar, and hydro producers to connect with investors, who are willing to pay upfront for the right to consume renewable energy. Blockchain makes a new energy-sharing economy possible, one that facilitates an open exchange of power between homes, with all transactions recorded through a decentralized ledger.

Gaming

The blockchain and gaming industries have maintained a significant demographic overlap since the inception of cryptocurrency. The concept of exchanging fiat currencies for digital currency or assets was already firmly established by multiplayer online games long before Satoshi Nakamoto published the bitcoin white paper. Gamers are largely adapted to digital economies, making the gaming industry an attractive environment to blockchain innovators and experimental platforms.

Examples and Use Cases

- *Crypto-collectibles*: A crypto-collectible is a cryptographically unique, nonfungible digital asset that has a limited quantity. Those who don't understand the appeal probably won't be any more interested, but much of it lies in novelty. Individuals who are now adults were in on the idea of digital pets back in the days, so the concept of trading blockchain-secured, unique digital assets has a broader audience than many may realize.

- *eSports betting*: eSports—a form of competition that revolves around video games—is an already impressive and growing sector of the gaming landscape. Individuals and teams seeking funding for their eSports careers can feel like needles in a haystack, but blockchain platforms have emerged and continue to arise that are aimed at connecting talented e-athletes with willing investors to mitigate the reliance upon traditional sponsorships.

- *Unique in-game assets*: In-game assets take several forms, and many developers create an opportunity for gamers to purchase those assets to continue replenishing their development budget. Systems used to pay for these assets have proven vulnerable to hacks, and the assets themselves aren't always truly unique. To solve these issues, the blockchain has been floated as a means to reduce duplicate content and also execute more secure transactions when purchasing and selling in-game assets.

Government

Blockchain technology can be used not only to capture votes to elect government officials, but also to operate the machine of governance itself. The state functions as a necessary centralized point of coordination in society and works primarily to establish laws and implement them. The democratic process, however, is burdened by multiple layers of redundancy, slow bureaucratic process, and red tape. Blockchain technology has many applications for the public sector, promising to improve communication, cut wastage, prevent fraud and corruption, and improve the quality of government services.

Examples and Use Cases

- *Combatting corruption*: In many countries, dishonest government individuals are the reason for corruption. Here, the blockchain will allow citizens to oversee government spending records, file and view specific complaints of corruption that cannot be whitewashed, publically register land and assets in nations where illegal confiscations are common, and create a system of transparent government contractors.

- *Customs and border patrol*: In many countries, customs and border patrol perform badly and will need to improve significantly to achieve the level of the better performers. That improvement could come from the adoption of blockchain technology, which will provide quicker, more reliable provenance about the origins and legitimacy of shipments, while also providing real-time records by which customs agents can plan and operate more efficiently. IBM and Maersk offer a platform to solve this problem.

- *Interagency data management*: Uniformity between centralized, siloed departments and the massive cobweb of varying bureaucratic standards and practices make the sharing of data and the processing of payments in government costly and nearly impossible. Establishing a single blockchain-based means of communication would protect from costly data breaches and losses, decrease training costs, reduce administrative costs, and establish a single standard by which the web of wasteful government spending could be shrunken.

- *Voting*: The blockchain is an ideal technology to end the polarized debate over the prevalence of voter fraud in the United States. Some states are already testing blockchain systems in local elections. The ability to vote on the Internet from home using blockchain technology will likely lead to greater participation thanks to greater convenience, while the immutable blockchain record can easily flag redundancies and tie unique personal identifiers to individuals to ensure that voters are who they say they are, and that they are eligible to vote.

Health care

Data interoperability is the biggest issue that faces the health care industry. Data released by Black Book Research demonstrates that 36 percent of health care professionals struggle with exchanging patient health care records between health care providers. The broad spectrum of electronic health care record providers and platforms and the disparity between the data standards used make it impossible for meaningful patient data to be shared outside of siloed medical data platforms. The U.S. Office of the National Coordinator for Health Information Technology's interoperability roadmap identifies a number of elements that are critical for healthcare interoperability. As you can see in Figure 3.5, the health care industry will be disrupting heavily.

Examples and Use Cases

- *Electronic health records (EHR)*: They were mandated under the Affordable Care Act, and they've seen a rocky rollout. Of surveyed physicians, 74 percent said their productivity either stayed the same or got worse for having to upkeep electronic records databases. Though less than 5 percent of health care providers have blockchain in their business plans, some believe they can solve EHR challenges with its help.

Figure 3.5 Blockchain and IoT in health care

Source: Healthcare Gazette24

- *Insurance records and reporting*: All Americans must have health insurance or face financial penalty. A total of 7.5 million tax filers faced a penalty in 2014, while another 12.5 million escaped a fine through an exemption. Some insurers are exploring how the blockchain's distributed ledger technology could record real-time changes to patient data. Such a system could help insurers and health care providers avoid massive fines due to archaic recordkeeping. It can also improve the quality of care for patients who switch providers or insurers..

- *Preventing fraudulent billing*: In 2016, $3.3 billion in health-care fraud judgments and settlements were collected, according to a report from the Department of Health and Human Services. That's not counting undiscovered fraud. Blockchain-based fraud prevention could lower administrative costs by automating claim processing and adjudication. It could also be a real-time record to monitor fraudulent claims more quickly and affordably.

- *Protecting patient data*: The cost of a single stolen record in the health care industry averaged $380 in the United States in 2017. It's a staggeringly high number compared to the global average of $141. Blockchain systems have multiple security checkpoints that minimize vulnerability. The technology could also give patients greater oversight of their own data through shared password-protected records.

- *Reducing counterfeit pharmaceuticals*: The World Health Organization (WHO) estimates that 10 percent of the world's pharmaceuticals are counterfeit. This puts $75 billion in the pockets of illegal drug manufacturers responsible for an estimated 100,000 deaths per year. These figures show why the blockchain is necessary as a unifying record for legal drug suppliers. A blockchain record would make the supply chain more accountable and help authorities identify fraudulent drugs more quickly.

Insurance

The insurance industry is also highly complex, consisting of brokers, insurers, consumers, and reinsurers, making the prediction of the industry's main product—risk—complicated. Insurance relies on a cumbersome, collaborative process that is fraught with hundreds of points of failure at which critical information can be lost, misinterpreted, or altered. Blockchain technology promises to solve the issues present in industries that rely heavily on the cooperation of multiple intermediaries driven by different motivators and incentives. Deloitte studies demonstrate a range of key benefits delivered by the blockchain that could dramatically transform the insurance industry.

Examples and Use Cases

- *Fraud prevention*: Insurers continue to be burned by fraudsters. One conservative estimate pegs the industry fraud losses at $80 billion per year. Higher premiums because of insurance fraud add up to $400 to $700 per year. Auto insurance represents the most costly form of insurance fraud; 25 percent of bodily injury claims resulting from car crashes are exaggerated or fraudulent. This adds up to $200 to $300 per year. If the blockchain can be used as the basis for an industry-wide store of information into which algorithms could be fashioned to detect repeat claims, chronic offenders, and other signs of fraud, it would be a major win.
- *Peer-to-peer insurance*: Peer-to-peer insurance is a relatively new term, but the roots of the industry go back to old-school mutual insurance. With a $64 billion valuation in 2015 and an anticipated value of $1 trillion by 2025, P2P insurance is on an undeniable upswing. It's clear to see why the market is expected to grow: members pool their resources, and unpaid premiums are returned to the members. This general vision

of insuring only what you need if you need it is being fitted
to blockchain technology, with members placing their funds
in digital wallets and those funds representing the amount of
exposure from which they are protected.

- *Property and casualty insurance*: Property and casualty insurance covers risk related to lost or damaged property, and it
  accounted for 47 percent of all premiums ($533.7 billion) writ-
  ten in 2016. With the blockchain, a completely new system
  of tracking the lifetime of an asset could be established. Smart
  contracts could digitize paper contracts and process claims
  based on coded criteria, calculating liabilities for all parties
  based on universal criteria and standards. Better yet, this record
  could be updated in real time by insurers and policyholders.

- *Reinsurance*: Reinsurance allows insurers to mitigate their risk
  by offloading policies on other insurers. Reinsurance expense
  ratios typically account for 5 to 10 percent of premiums.
  PricewaterhouseCoopers estimates that the introduction of
  blockchain technology in reinsurance could remove 15 to 25
  percent of expenses, delivering an industry-wide savings of
  $5 billion to $10 billion. The primary way to achieve these
  savings is through the adoption of a blockchain ledger.

- *Risk prevention*: The insurance industry is massive, consisting of over 7,000 companies collecting over $1 trillion in
  premiums annually. That makes the industry ripe for rip-off.
  Insurance companies have the duty of employing the most
  stringent risk prevention and fraud detection equipment,
  and the blockchain is at the frontier of cutting-edge fraud
  prevention tools. The technology can be utilized as a method
  to seamlessly and securely share fraud intelligence among
  decentralized institutions.

Manufacturing

Companies in the manufacturing industry have been pioneers of tech
innovation, driving trends like automation, digital transformation, and
supply chain modernization before they'd gained mainstream recognition.

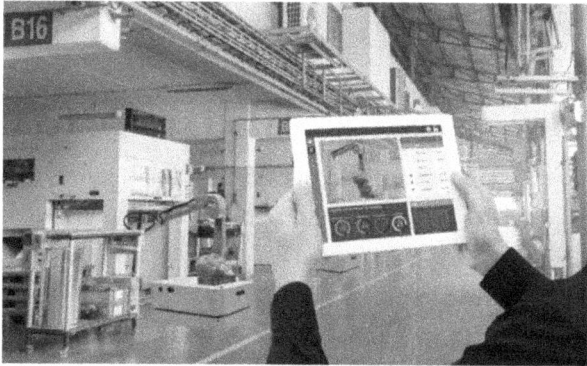

Figure 3.6 Blockchain of Things in manufacturing

Source: The Sociable

Blockchain could help manufacturers reduce the number of stops their products make on the way to the consumer. Most manufacturers have to go through countless intermediaries to get their products to the end user.

As factories become increasingly automated, we will begin to see more machine-to-machine interaction. Sooner than you think, this will result in machines that work for different organizations to interact with and potentially transact with one another. There is also an enormous amount of fraud in the industry that decentralized systems could mitigate. By creating more transparent tracking of goods and services, blockchain could help identify theft of products closer to the source of the theft. Manufacturing is one of the most impacted industries by the Blockchain of Things, as shown in Figure 3.6.

Examples and Use Cases

- *3D printing design rights*: Additive manufacturing, also known as 3D printing, has yet to achieve mainstream adoption, but the industry's momentum is heading in the right direction. The ability to provide a secure platform upon which 3D printing designs and instructions could be purchased or shared between parties is one of the blockchain's promises for the technology. Such a marketplace would allow 3D manufacturing designers a paying audience to sell their designs.

The blockchain has also proven good fit for handling financial transactions.

- *Improving trust in products*: According to one estimate, the cost of fraud globally in the manufacturing sector is $3.7 trillion, though that figure could easily rise as hackers continue to become more sophisticated and effective. The blockchain's decentralized technology could allow fraud information to be shared, but not compromised or altered.

- *IoT device authentication*: The IoT—the many connected devices and sensors that allow Big Data to be collected— is impacting most industries, including manufacturing. In fact, manufacturers rely heavily on utilizing logistical data to dissolve inefficiency and raise profits. IDC has predicted that by now, 75 percent of large manufacturers will have updated their operations with IoT devices to speed up the time to bring products to market. Providing a secure network by which IoT devices can be authenticated, monitored, and through which information can be secured is the primary use case intersection of blockchain and IoT.

- *Lowering barriers to entry*: Renewed dedication to the American manufacturing sector has created new opportunities for smaller manufacturers to gain a profitable foothold in the domestic market. According to CNBC, the 327,000 new jobs created in the manufacturing sector between July 2017 and July 2018 were the most in any 12-month period since April 1995. Utilizing the blockchain is one way to create value for a business seeking to make their name in manufacturing. A reported 58 percent of manufacturing companies utilized blockchain technology in 2017.

- *Production part approval process (PPAP)*: PPAP is an 18-element test for ensuring that parts meet requirements for their respective industry. Though this process was first utilized in the automotive and aerospace industries, it has become a staple of other manufacturing sectors. For each step of the PPAP, the blockchain can serve as an interoperable storage locker for necessary certifications. By creating uniformity of PPAP tests, the blockchain can contribute significantly to the evolution of manufacturing processes.

- *Supply chain auditing*: Seventy-eight percent of supply chain managers worry about supply chain disruptions, and anxiety can be particularly high in manufacturing. Between 2014 and 2017, supply chain waste and abuse fraud risk jumped from 25.2 to 35 percent. Manufacturers have fixed their eyes on blockchain, as a means to minimize supply chain disruption. Companies are working to perfect systems by which all participants on a supply chain refer to. These systems will allow manufacturers to curtail product loss and provide an unprecedented measure of provenance to those who they pass the finished product along to.

Marketing

Marketing is one of those vital budget line items that are always on the edge of being cut and always hard to quantify. Regardless of the industry, virtually every company has some kind of marketing spend to help connect their products and services with relevant customers. One of the challenges is that recording a customer's journey through a site may happen for the IT or marketing teams, but that data often gets siloed, when the entire organization could benefit from reviewing it. Blockchain-based platforms could help not only record the entire customer journey but make it readily accessible for all relevant partners.

Another way blockchain could help marketers is by giving them a tool to incentivize user and customer data sharing. Currently, there is a war between marketers and users, with users wanting to hold their data back and with marketers always wanting more of it. The blockchain is seen by many as a means to flip marketing on its head by providing better metrics for a wider audience, reducing the influence of data and audience-hoarding intermediaries, and transforming potentially effective marketing strategies such as loyalty programs through innovative approaches. How the Blockchain of Things is disrupting marketing can be seen in Figure 3.7.

Figure 3.7 Blockchain of Things in marketing

Source: Analytics Insight

Examples and Use Cases

- *Anonymity in marketing data collection*: Our Internet person-
  alities are essentially a glass house exposing our many interests
  and beliefs. While this is a treasure for marketers and retailers, it's created quite a bit of controversy, especially for those
  who believe that a free platform is free because of its creators'
  benevolence. Everyone recalls the hot water Facebook got
  itself into by being less than open about how it collects data,
  and they are not the only one. Blockchain practitioners begin
  establishing systems that anonymize user data. The anonymity
  could ensure that the data is not tied to any specific person.
  Other ventures are seeking to establish networks that prevent
  a user's data from being collected without their permission,
  and a peer-to-peer alternative in which user data is encrypted.
- *Consolidating gift card merchants*: Gift cards are a great
  marketing tool for businesses, as over 59 percent of surveyed
  consumers tend to spend more than the gift card's value once
  they go shopping. Gift cards are often applicable across the
  members of a parent company. So a system by which a greater
  number of businesses consolidate their offerings, allowing
  a customer to amass the sum of their gift card on a single
  debit-like gift card, could result in greater earnings for all

companies involved. The blockchain could serve as a secure locker for these gift cards, utilizing unparalleled authentication methods to tie a single user to their gift card sum, creating a more versatile, seamless means to take advantage of their credits.

- *Tokenizing loyalty rewards programs*: Loyalty programs are one of the most obvious differentiators that can compel a consumer to choose one place of business over another. As of 2017, 3.8 billion Americans possessed membership in at least one customer loyalty program. But still too many businesses fail to fully flesh out their programs. The blockchain could serve as a means to incentivize engagement by providing more immediate rewards. This concept has to do with the idea of making rewards programs unified on the blockchain so that customers could redeem their points in a more immediate manner or even trade the points to other members on the chain marketplace if they please.

- *Validating e-mail delivery*: E-mail remains an integral part of staying in touch, especially for professionals. In 2017, 3.7 billion Internet users relied upon e-mail as a form of communication. Countless e-mails get lost in the weeds with spam boxes and lack of oversight accounting for the immeasurable number of transmissions that go unread. For marketers, this is a problem. The blockchain, with its ability to collect metadata and track engagement, could provide the framework for the collection of metrics, which in turn would mean greater insight into how campaigns can be tweaked to better connect with the target audience.

- *Verifying engagement*: The Internet has become plagued with bots posing as humans, muddying up engagement statistics and costing publications and retailers valuable advertising dollars. Advertising fraud is nothing new. In 2013, Adweek published an article claiming that 20 to 90 percent of all clicks on online campaigns were executed by bots, not actual humans who might be inclined to visit an emergent news site or purchase the luxury patio furniture being advertised.

The blockchain has a great capability to weed out bots, ensuring that interactions are conducted by humans. This opens the door for a new paradigm in digital advertising, creating the potential for engagement to be truly verified.

Music

Experts project the music industry to grow from $1.4 billion to $17.2 billion between 2012 and 2021. That's a lot of growth! Centralized streaming media platforms, such as Spotify and YouTube, are commonly criticized for delivering insufficient remuneration to artists and creators. Blockchain technology offers a solution to the problem of artist remuneration.

Blockchain innovators are focused on narrowing the gulf between top earners and starving artists. Smart contract technology will make royalty payments and rights management more equitable. Technology will likely replace intermediaries, automating payment processes at a lower cost. The blockchain could also underpin a more secure platform for creatives to share their content in a way that discourages piracy. Some innovators envision entirely new ways to stream music using blockchain platforms.

Examples and Use Cases

- *Affordable music platforms*: Music piracy is more popular than ever, growing 14.7 percent between 2016 and 2017; 35 percent of music buyers occasionally download at least one song from an unsanctioned source. Plenty of people can't justify paying for music. The blockchain ledger automates processes to lessen the middlemen between music creators and consumers. Fewer DJs in the booth should produce a less costly song. In a perfect world, savings would trickle all the way down to the consumer.
- *Digital rights management*: Digital copyrights restrict exposure to new music. When people can't hear a new song, what will prompt them to purchase it? The record label EMI saw a 10 percent uptick in sales after removing copyright protection from their digital music. The music industry lacks a system for storing these rights accurately and securely. The block-

chain is secure and alterable, and might be a suitable frame-work for a musical rights management platform.

- *Fair trade databases*: Artists received only 12 percent of the $43 billion in sales generated by the music industry last year. How could the blockchain help musicians make money? A fair trade music database is loosely imagined as a public database where artists can upload their music and receive a large cut of the sales. Contracts prevent most artists from signing up for this sort of database immediately. It would have far greater appeal to unsigned artists. This is the major question mark: who will pay for broke, unsigned artists' database?

- *Micro payments for artists*: The top 1 percent of musicians earn 77 percent of revenue from recorded music. I'm talking about an industry where the big fish gobble up virtually all of the major contracts, air time, and fame. Some streaming services and record labels use micro payments. Some services pay artists each time their song plays by sending cryptocurrency to a digital wallet. The direct payment gateway cuts out inter-mediaries and lowers the cost of international transactions. It ensures that creatives receive fair earnings for their work.

- *Royalty systems*: Spotify paid a $30 million settlement in 2016 over unpaid royalties. The suit is evidence that digital music streaming hasn't ended the industry's financial quarrels. Royalty payments aren't cheap for streaming platforms either. They cost Spotify $1.9 billion in 2017. Industry-wide royalty tracking and payment powered by the blockchain will add transparency and value for all parties. It may also decrease royalty payment fees. Imagine paying rights holders as soon as songs are down-loaded, instead of weeks, months, or years later. Automated payment with smart contracts could make this a reality.

Retail

The key advantage offered by cryptocurrencies is the ability for users to immediately transact in a trustless manner without the need for third-party intermediaries. This advantage delivers obvious benefits to retail,

Figure 3.8 Blockchain and IoT in retail

Source: The Merkle Hash

providing retailers with the ability to accept cryptocurrencies in exchange for goods and services and dramatically reduce fiat processing and transaction fees. Blockchain technology makes it possible for both retailers and e-commerce operators to not only receive immediate, low-cost remittance for goods and services but execute postsale supply chain and distribution processes automatically with smart contract technology.

There are significant challenges facing the retail sector that could determine which players become long-term beneficiaries of evolution and which fall off the map completely. Online retailers were responsible for a significant portion of retail sale increases, which contributed 11 percent of the total increase in a one-month segment. Blockchain technology is uniquely equipped to deal with the challenges facing retailers, from providing greater oversight for supply chain management to offering the provenance and proof-of-ethicality that so many consumers now demand, and more. Retail, as in Figure 3.8, is impacted by Blockchain and IoT especially in inventory oversight.

Examples and Use Cases

- *Accepting crypto payments*: The vast majority of customers who could be incentivized to buy more, higher priced furnishings from crypto accepting retailers remain largely untapped. There are admittedly hurdles, such as the inclination of crypto investors to hold onto the assets when the price is appreciating, but analysts point out that eventually spending those coins will be necessary to cement their real-world value.

- *Consumer demand contracts*: Data shows us that consumers value convenience more than ever: 51 percent of Americans prefer to shop online, including 67 percent of millennials, and one-third of retailers stated that "targeting and personalization" was among their top three priorities for the year ahead. Through smart contract technology, consumers may be able to lay out a project and retailers would be able to bid to provide individual elements of the project. Smart contracts would handle the payment and shipment logistics for each retailer, who would have to fulfill specifications in order to fulfill the contract.

- *Customer identity*: There are benefits to sharing our browsing and purchase data with retailers: 56 percent of consumers are willing to share data to receive faster and more convenient service, and 64 percent of consumers want personalized offers from retail brands. The blockchain could serve as an easily accessible way for consumers to store and manage their retail-linked data, protecting it with permissions and sharing it only with retailers who convince them that sacrificing some measure of privacy is worth the payoff, whether financial or otherwise.

- *Preventing fraud and counterfeit goods*: Retail losses due to fraud in 2017 were estimated to incur at least $23 billion in losses. High-end retailers average 20 to 30 percent greater losses, especially due to high margins and lenient return policies. Blockchain technology and its ability to assign unique identifiers to each product is expected to provide unprecedented security in identifying counterfeit items in the supply chain, as well as immediately and cheaply rejecting fraudulent returns.

- *Product contracts*: Nearly 75 percent of retail procurement executives stated that, in an effort to increase their profits, they would rely upon supply chain technology to drive greater supplier efficiency. One proposed solution for incentivizing greater efficiency among suppliers is smart contract-facilitated product contracts, which provide payment promises for the fulfillment of supply chain-related milestones. These product contracts would provide suppliers with tangible motivation to meet higher speed and quality standards in delivering a shipment, which would ultimately result in greater profits for the retailer.

- *Supply chain/inventory oversight*: Regardless of a retailer's sub-sector, the ability to establish a more transparent supply chain for the customer has obvious benefits. All retailers can benefit from better product provenance tools, as consumers are increasingly concerned with the origins of their things, both from an ethical and a value-based standpoint. Beyond product losses and fraud prevention, transparency in retail supply chains via blockchain-distributed ledger technology will give early adopters a competitive advantage, and will likely become the industry standard in the long run.

Smart Cities

Smart cities went through a pretty big hype cycle about two years back, and now you don't hear about them as often. That's largely due to the fact that many of the innovation and government-based grants are currently underway testing out smart city concepts and building the first infra-structures required for a more connected civic future. The modern smart city already constitutes a massive web of interconnected technologies, and that web is expected to grow rapidly, with Gartner projecting that 9.7 billion IoT devices will make up the typical smart city by 2020.

Blockchain technology can provide much of the digital infrastructure that will be required for smart cities to become a reality. So while munic-ipalities and tech leaders are working on building exciting IoT hardware, they should also be considering the future of interoperability, automa-tion, and how blockchain can create protocols and security for connected

Figure 3.9 Blockchain of Things in smart cities

Source: Smart Cities World

systems. It may also serve as a reputation management tool, as these cities tend to be chock-full of citizens who demand a certain standard from individuals and businesses when it comes to communal and environmental care.

What a smart city looks like can be seen in Figure 3.9.

Examples and Use Cases

- *Departmental transparency*: While 37 percent of Internet users report using the web to find information about their federal government, just 5 percent say that their government is effective in sharing information with the public. However, 66 percent of American respondents held hope that a greater network of open data will improve government accountability. Information to which the voting public should be privy could be logged on the blockchain and made accessible through widely accessible apps. A single source of secure, verified information would eliminate much of the confusion and misinformation that arises from the current system of information disseminated via the Internet.

- *Improving public transit*: Public transit ridership has increased 26 percent over the past 20 years, and the emergence of more smart cities and their highly localized economies has been predicted to incentivize greater reliance on public transit. The blockchain has been proposed as a single point of payment for the various types of public transport, including bus, train, and subway tickets The uniformity of the platform would plausibly allow the preloading of funds on a card, and a person who utilized both a train and a bus ride on the same trip could pay via a single transaction. More uses for the blockchain in public transport are almost certain to arise.

- *Interoperability for smart devices*: Interoperability is an essential feature of smart devices, with 75 percent of surveyed consumers stating that it is essential that their smart devices used within the home connect seamlessly to other products in their home electronic network. Currently, 32 percent of U.S. households with access to broadband own at least one smart connected device. The blockchain represents a single platform upon which a very smart individual or company will create a secure, interoperable control system for the massive and growing web of smart devices.

- *Keyless signature interface (KSI)*: In 2016, there were 30,899 information security incidents pertaining to the breach of government data, 16 of which qualified as major incidents. KSI is a form of blockchain established in Estonia and put to use by the Estonian government. It provides permanent records of timestamping that render the data immutable, whether attempts are made by hackers or system administrators. This means a high level of transparency and permanence for government records, which is a valuable asset in any setting where government accountability is required, including smart cities.

- *Rewarding citizenship*: Ten percent of all children and 15 percent of poor children in the United States live in mixed status families, meaning that proactive, outside-the-box solutions to solving an immigration and legal status debate should be welcomed. Some are looking to the blockchain as a new, incentive-driven approach to attaining citizenship. Programs in which citizens can trade data about themselves and their needs are being launched to cater smart cities to the lives of their citizens. These programs also require strong personal identification aspects, meaning that presumably only citizens would dictate which projects are undertaken.

- *Security for IoT devices*: The global cost of cyber-security crime is anticipated to hit $6 trillion by 2021, and the heightened interconnectivity of devices comprising the IoT in smart cities could make this damage exponential in nature. That's why 47 percent of IoT developers cite security as their primary concern. The more data we collect, the more difficult it becomes to secure the ever-growing store of potentially sensitive information. Considering the sheer amount of data that will be utilized by IT systems in smart cities, this data gold mine—and potentially city-crippling vulnerability—must be protected by a technology worthy of these high stakes: the blockchain.

- *Universal data storage platforms*: What we have gained in terms of convenience and storage capacity has come at a cost, namely, security. The average cost of a data breach for a U.S. enterprise in 2017 was $1.3 million, and $117,000 for small and medium-sized businesses. The confluence of data that will be collected and interlinked in smart cities—sensor data, smart grid data, smart vehicle data, and so on—cannot be compromised by being stored on a centralized, easily assailable data hub. The blockchain serves as the only suitable option to provide both interoperability and security to a universal data storage platform catered to life in smart cities.

Supply Chain and Logistics

The supply chain, which consists of a complex system of relationships between manufacturers, suppliers, retailers, and customers, is an integral element of global commerce. The supply chain network, however, is highly centralized, with third parties managing virtually every step of the supply chain process. Supply chain managers who embrace technology may see an exponential growth effect, because digital business planning solutions can lower product innovation costs by 10 percent, in turn reducing new product lead times by 30 percent.

Applied to the supply chain industry, distributed ledger networks not only confirm payment, but also track goods in transport, confirm delivery status, and track warehousing. One of the most interesting applications of blockchain technology in the supply chain industry is the use of smart contracts. In the case of the supply chain, smart contracts can be used, for example, to trigger the delivery of an order once payment is recorded on the blockchain. Other ways that the blockchain can benefit supply chain managers and their companies include greater transparency and accountability between suppliers; a ledger of manifests, departure, and arrival times; and a reduction in human error across the board thanks to more widespread automation. An overview of the transformation caused by the Blockchain of Things can be found in Figure 3.10.

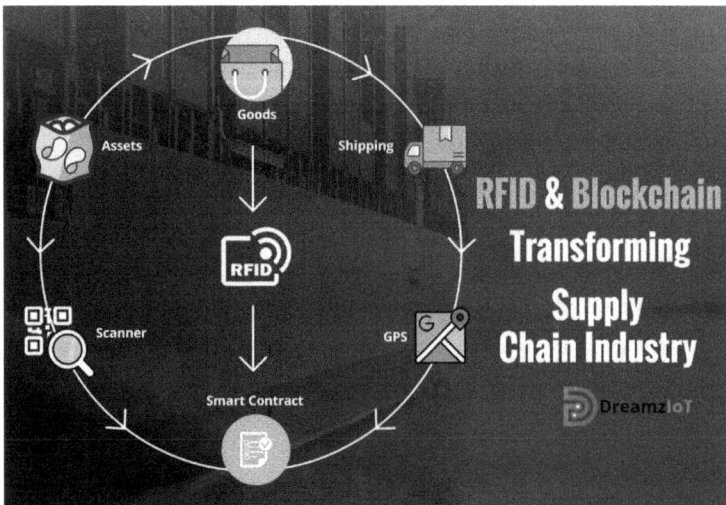

Figure 3.10 Blockchain of Things in supply chain

Source: DreamzIoT

Examples and Use Cases

- *Better shipping data*: One survey showed that 89 percent of consumers worry about receiving a product late, and 83 percent have concerns that the product will be damaged. In order to improve this, 90 percent of respondents said that real-time data access and better information sharing systems are needed, including 82 percent who said the industry needed to improve supply chain visibility. The blockchain's shared, decentralized ledger technology is just perfect for the job, providing a uniform mode of recordkeeping that is interoperable by all players in a supply chain and can be updated in real time.

- *Food safety*: Although the United States is one of the most food safety-conscious nations in the world, there are still 48 million cases of foodborne illness each year, the equivalent of 1 in 6 Americans being made ill. The severe health consequences of mismanagement in food supply chains—consequences that can cause major, potentially irreconcilable disruptions in one's personal and professional life—necessitate that significant steps be made to enhance transparency in the industry.

- *Preventing compliance violations*: A civil penalty for a violation of American trade compliance laws can run up to $1 million, 20 years imprisonment per violation, and additional penalties of up to $250,000 per transaction. The blockchain is precisely the decentralized, interoperable record that supply chain managers don't just desire, but need, to avoid massive fines and potential jail time.

- *Provenance*: Whether in art, food service, pharmaceuticals, or elsewhere, the tangible value of provenance is undeniable: in England, international consumers were prepared to pay 22 percent more for British-made goods. By the end of 2018, only 17 percent of companies won't be considering or employing some level of supply chain automation. Considering the value that customers, distributors, and retailers put on provenance, blockchain tech has the ability to record every transaction on a permanent record. Consumers yearn for provenance now more than ever, and with the blockchain we have the tools to deliver that demand.

- *Reducing human error*: Manual processes inherent to supply chain management are notoriously prone to human error. Even the most careful, skilled data entrants typically see a 2 percent error rate, or 20 cells in a 200-cell Excel spreadsheet. Margins in the logistics sector are low already, if they exist at all, typically ranging between –1 and 8 percent. Blockchain supply management platforms are designed to reduce reliance on humans, instead automating transactions, recordkeeping, data entry, and inventory tracking systems in a way that is faster and more affordable.

- *Tracking social responsibility*: Eighty-six percent of consumers expect companies to act on social and environmental issues. They're also willing to do their part, with 81 percent of consumers stating that they will make personal sacrifices to address social and environmental issues. The blockchain's ability to trace products' progress along a supply chain provides a record that allows easy access to each specific product, proving that the product's path to shelf was not forged on the back of children or other unethical means.

- *Transaction settlement*: In 1999, GE saved $1.8 billion by digitizing its payment settlement processes. Time-consuming cross-border payments, which are routine in many supply chains, drain $1.6 trillion in system-wide costs per annum. The blockchain allows for faster transaction settlement by (a) processing payments directly from peer to peer with no third-party intervention, (b) automatically and immediately updating ledgers, and (c) executing both ends of a transaction simultaneously.

Telecoms

Telecom Industry's evolution has helped to gain the digital world where we live today, yet the technological revolution is continually changing and the industry is trying to match up the need of the public. Telecom industry today has the most complex operations frameworks. It involves partners, vendors, customers, distributors, network providers; the involvement of multiple entities has increased the difficulty even more. Besides them, there are many other challenges faced by the telecom industry such as decrease in voice revenue, development of 5G, and security of the network.

Blockchain is one of the innovative technological innovations that can truly bring changes to the telecommunication industry and ultimately assist in the business model transformation. It can advance strategic objectives that lay the foundation for a digital economy network and ultimately transform its business model. Different countries have adopted the blockchain technology in the telecom industry for achieving its maximum advantages. The early adopters are certain to benefit in several ways in the future.

Examples and Use Cases

- *Digital identity*: The security of the networks is one of the major issues faced by telcos. Finding the solution to the emergence of new threats powered by the new technologies has become the highest priority of the telecom industry. Blockchain can establish a secure record of the identities for the people, assets, personal devices and also has the ability to connect with the IoT sensors. The decentralized ledger could reduce the fraud and strengthen the trust between the transacting parties. On the same way, the proper detection of identity can be used to minimize the fraud, track the overall content, and direct the proper royalties.
- *Dynamic and high-performing 5G networks*: 5G, the latest generation of cellular mobile communication, is supposed to improve the capacity and latency along with an increase in the speed of the spectrum. It will also facilitate the development of IoT by completely transforming the mobile technology. The 5G networks along with the dynamic connectivity of billions of devices across an array of the access point, includ-

ing vehicles and the smart cities, make it quite complex. The delay faced by telcos to build complicated 5G networks can be accelerated using the blockchain. Telcos using the stronger blockchain network can take an industry-wide approach and update their network infrastructure and transactional ecosystem.

- *Fraud prevention*: There is over $38 billion loss annually due to the existing fraud in the industry. The complexity of the telecom network and its vulnerability makes it hard for the detection of fraud and on the other hand, the telecom industry has not yet found an effective and sustainable solution to address this major problem. Blockchain technology along with its ability to detect fraud can be used in abolishing the prevalent frauds.

- *Online security*: Online security is one of the global concerns. Blockchain technology runs with the decentralization concept and supports the secure transaction removing the risk element and guaranteeing the transparency. All the transactions are stored in the ledger which could be verified easily since the transactions stored in blockchain are encrypted, time-stamped, and synchronized with the entire network. Anyone trying to alter the records could be caught red-handed easily. The nature of blockchain makes everyone in the chain to have full control over the data eliminating the single person's authority.

- *Rid of middleman*: The prevalent middleman at various levels requires the service charge accordingly increasing the expenses of the industry. Blockchain technology cuts off the involvement of any middleman; telcos could benefit easily from blockchain and save a huge amount of money. According to the communications service provider CIO from the United States, "Blockchain will provide a secure platform, the possibility to omit third-party intermediaries, and security measures against fraud and cybercrime."

- *Securing and managing IoT networks*: There are many cases where telcos are becoming the leading IoT service provider.

With blockchain, a great level of security and automated management of device identity, authorization, provision, and transactions are possible. The main advantages of this integration are the decrease in authentication times and a simultaneous increase in the potential of demand-based revenue streams for the device data. Blockchain can minimize the attack surface of vulnerabilities while smart contract extends the provision of failing or compromised devices.

Transportation

Ride-sharing apps, such as Uber, represent the pinnacle of Web 2.0-based decentralization, allowing anybody with a vehicle to participate in the transport economy on a mercenary basis. Bringing ride-sharing platforms onto the blockchain completely eliminates the middlemen that elevate prices, allowing individuals to connect directly to drivers who are willing to transport them in a completely decentralized manner. The way how the Uber app is being used already can be seen in Figure 3.11.

A blockchain-based ride-sharing app would attach metadata such as location and reviews to a user profile published on the blockchain,

Figure 3.11 Blockchain of Things in transportation Uber

Source: The Sun

allowing the blockchain to filter and match platform participants, transport users, and autonomously execute payment via smart contract. There are several ways that blockchain technology will assist the public transportation. It could secure fleets of rented bike, help coordinate ride sharing, and disseminate critical data—as a start to its potential use cases.

Examples and Use Cases

- *Decentralized nontraditional transportation services*: Look at a city you consider to be progressive and you're likely to see a disproportionate number of public transportation users. Not just regular old bus riders, but bike and scooter riders, too. Among the most bike-friendly cities are Amsterdam, Portland, Copenhagen, Tokyo, and Barcelona. The blockchain could facilitate the rewarding riders with tokens, tickets, and other rewards for using public transportation. This will help speed the movement toward nontraditional modes of public transportation as a mainstream way of getting around.

- *Maintenance data tracking and safety*: When you're driving your own vehicle, you have the peace of mind of knowing you did have the oil changed, the brake pads are up to date, and it's generally safe to operate. With public transportation, that peace of mind is hardly as apparent. You should be able to safely assume that buses aren't driving around their city with faulty brakes or a combustible engine. The blockchain could also be a vehicle to issue automated alerts and usage reports for fleets of public vehicles. These benefits would take much of the burden off public and private employees, who are often forced to rely on outdated maintenance systems.

- *Mobility as a service economy*: Many believe the economy will benefit from the further growth of ridesharing, autonomous vehicles, and public transport. The concept of Mobility-as-a-Service (MaaS) is a better, faster, more connected, and personal transportation that can bring benefits to cities, communities, and transit agencies. The European Union's MaaS Alliance goes further, stating that MaaS is the integration of various forms of transport into a single mobility service accessible on demand.

- *Transparent public transportation data*: Knowing how well public transport vehicles are functioning is key to a system running smoothly and sustainably. One of the strongest arguments for broadening the use of public transportation is an overall decrease in pollution emissions. But vehicles have to be up to environmental and performance standards for that goal to be realized. A database of information about public transportation fleets on the blockchain will increase public awareness. Because blockchain ledgers are immutable and permanent, they are suited for publicly consumable information.

- *Universal transit payment systems*: The process for obtaining and utilizing tickets, especially across different modes of public transport, is often fragmented and time-consuming. Those who want to ride multiple trains, hop on a bus, and then rent a bike might need to execute four different transactions. There are plenty of reasons to shun public transport already. Creating more efficient systems for ticketing helps get riders back. Through blockchain-linked platforms and unique "mobility" coins, purchasing and applying tickets for public transportation becomes simpler. No longer visiting multiple ticketing desks or kiosks. Instead, a single platform for the purchase and storage of digital tickets will replace outdated processes.

Chapter Takeaways

- This chapter provides an overview of 17 industries and verticals that are being disrupted by the Blockchain of Things.
- Very disrupted industries include automotive, banking and financial services, energy, government, health care, manufacturing, and supply chain and logistics.
- The automotive industry is showing signs of profound change especially because of autonomous driving.

- Traditional banks and financial services are heavily investing in these technologies.
- The possibilities for the intersection of Blockchain of Things, energy, and sustainable technologies are staggering.
- The Blockchain of Things has many applications for the public sector including improvement of government services.
- Data interoperability in the health care industry is one of the biggest issues being improved by the Blockchain of Things.
- Blockchain of Things could help manufacturers reduce the number of stops their products make on the way to the consumer.
- The Blockchain of Things benefits supply chain managers and their companies with greater transparency and accountability between suppliers.

Management Questions for Your Business

- What industry or vertical does our company belong to?
- What use cases and main processes related to the Blockchain of Things do we want to implement?
- How will you describe processes, benefits and risks, security, and budgets for hardware, software, and personnel?
- How will you forecast tangible and intangible results or savings?
- What are the forecasted costs or budgets and forecasted results or savings of all use cases and main processes?
- What are the use cases or main processes with the highest positive cash flow?

References and Additional Reading

Campanella, D. 2018. *The Impact of Blockchain Technology on Capital Markets: A Transformation of our Financial System?* Munich, Germany, Studylab.
Sarsar, M. (2019) *The Big Disruption: IoT, Smart Cities, Connected Vehicles, Big Data Analytics: A Practitioner Point of View and Return of Experience,* Independently Published
www.cbp.gov

www.disruptordaily.com/
www.entrepreneur.com
www.federalreserve.gov/
www.healthit.gov/
www.localharvest.com
www.medium.com
www.sciencedirect.com/
www.sharedmobility.news/
www.ups.com
www.warehouseanywhere.com/

CHAPTER 4

Blockchain of Intelligent Things

In this chapter I highlight business opportunities and also business challenges driven by technologies such as the blockchain, Internet of Things (IoT), and artificial intelligence (AI). I like to call the convergence of these technologies the Blockchain of Intelligent Things (BoIT).

BoIT is becoming increasingly ubiquitous in the world around us and, as a result, is changing the behavior and expectations of employees, suppliers, and customers. In order to remain relevant in a rapidly evolving world, businesses need to evolve their business processes, people, and services to keep pace.

Businesses need to prepare for the inevitability of change as we head toward a data-driven economy. People see how smart and intuitive the applications on their phone are and expect the same level of intelligence in all of their interactions, albeit with a service provider like a bank or the software they use at the office.

It all comes down to using data better to connect with people and to make it easier for them to connect with you, and with the BoIT you enable that. These technological and other challenges are all set to impact businesses in potentially unimagined ways. Technologies such as automation and AI are already having a seismic impact on all industries as companies race to remain relevant.

Figure 4.1 shows the convergence of blockchain, IoT, and AI using data as a backbone.

Four main trends are expected to emerge from the current spate of change, and businesses that meet them will succeed in this new emerging world.

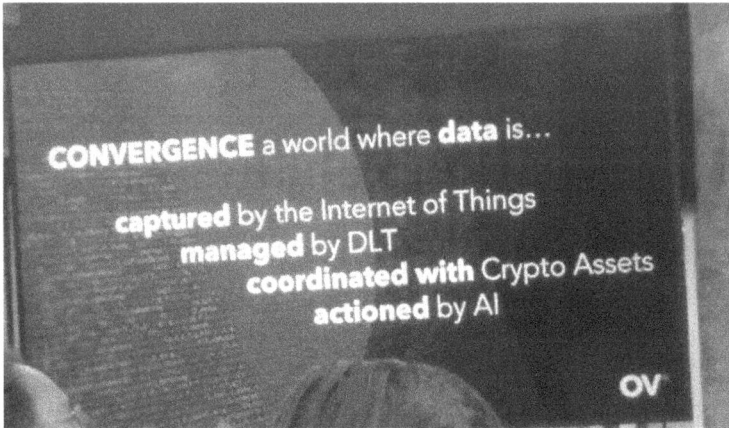

Figure 4.1 Blockchain of Intelligent Things

Source: SAP Blogs

- Going forward, everything has to be about the customer. A new generation has new expectations, and businesses must deliver on these if they want to remain relevant. This applies equally to customers and employees.
- The competition is no longer known; anyone can become a competitor as the boundaries between industries blur and previously diverse businesses partner to offer their customers more.
- The fourth industrial revolution is changing the way that businesses work and interact with one another, their suppliers, and their customers.
- The nature of risk is changing, with cyber-attacks on data becoming the new battleground.

It's all about having the right business model in place as well as intelligent platforms to turn these challenges into opportunities. More than this, these have to be able to adapt on the fly to keep pace with evolutions peripheral to your industry that may still impact your business. Flexibility and agility are key, with decisions being made on up-to-date data.

It all adds up to having the right partnerships in place, staying abreast of the latest technology developments, while keeping your business advantage.

We can identify four broad imperatives for any business looking to optimize how technology can add value to their organization:

1. Understand how to use the information available to provide strategic insight in real time.
2. Maximize the use of technology to think forward.
3. Implement effective and efficient processes that satisfy the overall business requirements.
4. Capture, measure, report, and predict future performance in a much more agile manner to support better and faster decision making.

This is where preparation and readiness will pay off. The sooner businesses see the digital transformation challenge as one of processes and people instead of as purely technological in nature, the sooner they'll make progress on their journey. We have to be ready for what lies ahead, and the one rule that holds true across all businesses and industries is that collaboration is going to be key going forward.

The attack surface and impacts of cyber-security events continue to grow at a staggering pace. The threat landscape leads to an important question that applies to everyone at every level of an organization. How do you help shield your organization from cyber-security threats?

The threats faced by organizations may include attacks from skilled and advanced attackers, but the broad swath of attempts from commodity malware, ransomware, viruses, opportunistic hacking, social engineering, and the numerous other commonplace threat types continue to be a nemesis for many organizations.

No matter the current state of your security program, there are ways in which you can build stronger defenses to thwart these attempts or mitigate the potential damage.

Business Value of Data Science

If you are in the process of figuring out exactly what benefits of data science for business have value to your company, you can consider the following ways of using data science:

- *Automating repetitive, time-consuming processes*: Automation is one of the hottest trends in modern technology. So, let's discuss applications of data science in business for creating automated innovations. To identify growth opportunities that automation can bring to your company, you can start by asking yourself:
  - ○ Where do people in my company spend a lot of time to make decisions that could be automated, so their skills could be better leveraged elsewhere?
  - ○ What types of data do people in my company normally search for and collect manually, and how can this be automated?
  - ○ Which tasks in my company can machines perform faster and more efficiently than humans?
- *Building better products*: By using data science in business, you can bring a better product to your target market in two main ways: you can either customize a product or service to make it more personal or you can provide a new experience with the product or service. Today data science looks most attractive for businesses in terms of generating real value and enabling break-through innovation. There are three main types of AI algorithms:
  - ○ *Unsupervised learning*: Allows you to capture your customer preferences and use the data to anticipate their needs and behaviors in the future. The most common examples of unsupervised learning are Amazon's recommendations based on what other customers also bought.
  - ○ *Supervised learning*: Used in predicting customer behavior. By solving a classification problem, machine learning engineers may help you identify satisfied and unsatisfied customers and predict churn.
  - ○ *Reinforcement learning*: Reinforcement learning refers to goal-oriented algorithms, in which an "agent" learns to accomplish a specific objective or goal. RL agents are what people often think of when they describe AI as portrayed in movies. The RL agent, under the right conditions, can achieve amazing performances as it learns about its environment.

- *Making better decisions*: With data science and predictive analytics, in particular, you can predict useful metrics and trends for your business. Such an approach can help you improve your ability to serve your customers or otherwise compete in the market. The importance of data science and predictive analytics is in the fact that organizations can leverage the power of technology to detect what can negatively impact businesses before these issues happen or spread. Predictive analytics is all about connecting disparate systems and data sets to do proper analysis and derive valuable insight out of seemingly chaotic data.

Examples per Industry

The BoIT is turning quite a few industries upside down. Convergence of Industrial IoT (IIoT) and AI, introduction of Cobots, and usage of augmented reality are some of the significant trends in BoIT applications in Industry 4.0. Statistics associated with the deployment of IIoT solutions indicate that early adopters will be able to generate five times more revenue than late adopters. Companies should ideally focus on narrowing down the business value drivers they are looking to contribute to. This way, they can position their digital strategy with their business goals to utilize IoT platforms efficiently.

Automotive

Here are the biggest ways the BoIT is transforming the automotive industry and our roads, including the topic of self-driving cars:

- *BoIT will change the way people drive: By 2030 the standard car will have evolved* from assisting drivers to fully taking control. Apart from widespread automation, cars will become more integrated through BoIT technology. Integrated cars with sensors will be able to recognize and communicate with upgraded road signs, markings, and through a network of cameras. The vehicles will also be able to do tasks for drivers.

- *BoIT can improve road safety:* The BoIT can also be used to make roads safer through alerts that detect accidents and even bad driving. There are already devices that automatically detect collisions and immediately contact emergency services with the location. The same technology can also provide a report to the vehicle's manufacturer so they can make any improvements. The majority of accidents on the road are down to human error, and these could be reduced through BoIT technology. This is because it can be used to monitor driving habits and send recommendations to the driver.

- *BoIT can help solve traffic congestion in cities:* The BoIT enables traffic operators to coordinate cars in order to reduce congestion. They can see where common chokepoints are, and identify the time of day when roads are busiest. This information can help engineers and road experts devise plans that can alleviate traffic conditions.

- *BoIT can help reduce pollution and energy expenditure:* BoIT data can reveal a lot of information about city roads, which can be used to create greener solutions. Let's take the example of Singapore, as the city aggressively implements congestion charges, not to mention their intent focus on investing in road sensors, phased traffic lights, and smart parking. These BoIT-driven tools have helped them reduce the city's toxic gas emissions.

- *BoIT will lead to better roads:* With the BoIT, state and local departments are able to build roads that can help detect road maintenance needs, traffic usage, and accident statistics in a matter of seconds. This will ensure that roads are not left in a poor condition for extended periods of time. In the future BoIT technology will also allow engineers to turn roads into energy sources by using solar energy to power electric vehicles. This will further increase the chances of electric vehicles becoming the norm.

Figure 4.2 Blockchain of intelligent things in automotive

Source: Business 2 Community

The BoIT is heavily disrupting the automotive industry while creating all kinds of innovations as you can see in figure 4.2.

"Self-driving" is a rather vague term with a vague meaning. I would like to mention the "self-driving levels" as defined by the SAE International. This means the vehicle can safely drive itself under specific conditions but the driver will need to quickly intervene when called on. This is a car that could drive itself on the highway while you watch a movie but would need you to take control when you get off the highway. Some may view this as only partially self-driving. Levels are defined as follows:

- *Level 1 automation:* Some small steering or acceleration tasks are performed by the car without human intervention, but everything else is fully under human control.
- *Level 2 automation:* It is like advance cruise control or original autopilot system on some Tesla vehicles; the car can automatically take safety actions but the driver needs to stay alert at the wheel.
- *Level 3 automation:* It still requires a human driver, but the human is able to put some "safety-critical functions" to the vehicle, under certain traffic or environmental conditions. This poses some potential dangers as humans pass the major tasks of driving to or from the car itself, which is why some

car companies (Ford included) are interested in jumping
directly to level 4.

- *Level 4 automation* is a car that can drive itself almost all the
  time without any human input, but might be programmed
  not to drive in unmapped areas or during severe weather. This
  is a car you could sleep in.
- *Level 5 automation* means full automation in all conditions.

Since these levels don't mean much to people outside the industry, car
makers often don't talk about their technology in these specific SAE
terms. The big potential promise for people is either cars that drive themselves for a large part of a person's highway commute (level 3) or cars that
can drive themselves almost as long as you live in a covered metropolitan
area (level 4).

Customer Services

When Francis Bacon first said "knowledge is power" he couldn't have
foreseen the extent to which his words would prove true in the digital age.
Today, business success comes not just from obtaining information, but
also from leveraging it in impactful ways. In customer service, this means
using holistic customer data to achieve the following:

- *Informed ticket classification*: The more data you have, the
  better your AI will function. With BoIT in customer service,
  AI-powered ticket classification will be increasingly accurate
  and "smart"—for example, routing to the best agent for the
  issue, balancing ticket backlog per agent, and suggesting
  knowledge base articles for ticket deflection. Brands that
  invest in AI-powered ticket routing now will have a huge leg
  up on competition when IoT in customer service becomes
  more mainstream.
- *Integrated cross-platform/device service*: IoT refers to the ability
  for devices to talk with one another. As customers increasingly
  rely on this capability, it will become more and more important for customer service to provide the same cross-device

continuity as consumers have with their everyday technology. This means enabling cross-device messaging (i.e., starting a conversation on a smartphone and continuing it on a laptop) and enabling cross-platform resolutions.

- *Smart issue resolution based on comprehensive customer journeys:* Not only does a wealth of data make AI more effective, but it also makes humans more effective. The more information that agents have on their customers' journeys, the easier it will be to identify issues and provide fast and effective resolutions. Features that enable agent collaboration and continuous conversations are important for offering a seamless customer experience (CX) throughout the customer journey.

Microsoft created a four-step flow to visualize intelligent customer services, as shown in Figure 4.3.

Energy

BoIT is becoming an increasingly popular presence in the energy sector. Through BoIT platforms, energy operators, distributors, and consumers can learn a lot about their habits and gain deep insights that could lead to several improvements along the way. Some of the most noticeable include:

- *Autonomous production*: In what surely is the most impressive of BoIT uses in the energy sector, there are experts

Figure 4.3 Intelligent customer services

Source: Microsoft

that predict that there'll come a day when wind and solar farms could be built and run without the need for humans. Through a combination of self-driving vehicles and BoIT robots, these farms could be assembled in less time and run 24/7 by BoIT-powered agents.

- *Better distribution*: Grid operators are using BoIT to assess thousands of variables that come into play in energy distribution and consumption. Thus, factors such as fluctuating demand, changing weather conditions, equipment failures, and end-user energy input to the grid are analyzed by complex algorithms to predict the energy demand and anticipate potential problems throughout the grid.

- *Enhanced maintenance scheduling*: BoIT is used to anticipate the equipment's wear and tear and even predict when the said equipment could break up or fail. In addition, through the analysis of sensors located throughout the production and distribution lines, BoIT is capable of creating an enhanced maintenance schedule. By doing that, it will be possible to repair any component of the grid before it breaks down, extending the whole system's life cycle and avoiding costly blackouts.

- *More efficient consumption*: BoIT is also being used to track domestic energy consumption to provide a detailed report on what appliances use up the most energy and the costs they generate. Beyond the somewhat limited current smart meters, there are solutions that take advantage of machine learning to identify the "energy vampires" in their user's homes and offer improvements that could cut energy use by about 10 percent.

- *Optimized energy production*: There are lots of ways in which BoIT can help in energy production—and several real cases to prove it. For instance, there are BoIT-powered adaptive controllers capable of suggesting optimizations in oil and gas as well as through sample analysis. Chevron is also using BoIT to find the best locations to drill new wells.

Health Care

Over the next decade, health care is expected to see a huge amount of technological change. BoIT is expected to play a huge role. A report by a company owned by Hewlett-Packard argued that the health care industry will need to embrace digital transformation. BoIT technologies are bound to be part of the mix. The study makes five key predictions for how the industry will transform by 2030, including:

- *Digital data repositories*: Devices will automatically integrate with your digital patient records, automatically updating on your condition and treatment, giving caregivers richer, real-time, readily accessible data to make better decisions.
- *Growth of AI*: As AI starts to play an increasing role in diagnosis and treatments, public support will grow to the extent that you will be willing to be diagnosed by machine, provided that services are designed and implemented around patients, the benefits are explained, and permission is sought.
- *Health professionals double their free time*: Doctors and nurses, who are currently spending up to 70 percent of their time on administrative work, will be able to quickly analyze scans or patient records via their mobile device, freeing up huge amounts of their day to focus on patient care.
- *Patient self-diagnosis*: Using app-based and wearable tools to monitor your health and even carry out your own scans, patients will finally have the ability to self-diagnose a wide number of conditions at home, without needing to visit a surgery or hospital.
- *The automated hospital*: Hospital check-in will feature imaging technology that can assess your heart rate, temperature, and respiratory rate from the moment you walk in. This will be followed by sensors that can perform a blood pressure and ECG test within 10 seconds and lead to an automatic triage or even diagnosis right then and there.

In health care we are seeing a massive push toward AI, analytics IoT, and robotics and the opportunities they can provide. From a patient management perspective, we want to drive preventative care to keep patients well in the first place and out of the hospital system. By having sensors and support tools in people's homes and feeding into analytics and AI, we can monitor their health remotely. On the analytics side, we have a push toward machine learning, allowing clinicians to act and take actions to deliver preventative and proactive care needed to make our system sustainable.

Logistics, Distribution, and Operations

BoIT is creating an intelligent supply chain, which you can see in Figure 4.4.

BoIT is changing logistics in the following ways:

- *Accurate information processing:* There is so much data floating around in a B2B company that if it is not identified and segmented properly, there will be chaos. For example, making sure that the information of the customer is correct can itself be a huge job. Validating the products ordered and matching

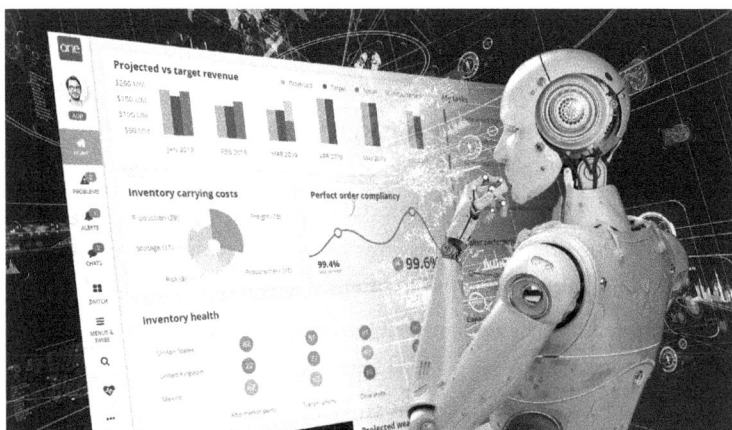

Figure 4.4 Intelligent supply chain

Source: The Network Effect

it to the specific customer can be a daunting task. BoIT makes all of this simple by validating the information in seconds.

- *Big Data*: The number of ways Big Data can benefit mankind is only getting bigger. The data that you get in logistics is not always refined, which is where AI comes into play by using algorithms to clean the data. Big Data with AI helps predict shipping volumes and plan for the future based on historical data. It will take into account other factors like weather and political landscape and make such decisions.

- *BoIT assists in last-mile delivery:* The focus of last-mile delivery is to ensure that the goods reach the customer as fast as possible. When an order is placed, there should be a system to ensure that the product is sent through the right channels, is packaged properly, and a delivery time range is informed to the customer and so on. BoIT makes this an extremely smooth affair by managing the different data points and assigning the executive as well as predicting the time it takes for the order to finally reach the customer.

- *BoIT helps with demand forecasting*: One of the most game-changing aspects of BoIT in logistics is going to be its ability to predict demand, optimize delivery routes, and manage networks. The predictive analytics part of AI helps companies make significant changes to their business based on the patterns that AI digs. Its ability to objectively measure the factors that lead toward efficiency helps its prediction in demand accuracy.

- *Creates contingency plans:* Like most aspects of life, the uncertainty of things going completely haywire in business is expected too. It is hard to be extremely well prepared in terms of exigencies that are beyond your control. BoIT is trained in such a way that it can not only prepare for exigencies but also predict the best method to tackle such situations. It can also work on corrective measures so that such situations can be avoided in the future.

- *Intelligent warehousing:* Online grocer Ocado's Andover (England) warehouse is entirely run by robots. It fulfills more than 65,000 orders (or about 3.5 million grocery items) every week. The robots, using BoIT, move, lift and segregate the items which are then packed by the employees. It ensures that the entire space is utilized by stacking boxes high by keeping up to 17 of them on top of each other. The AI is so smart that items which are rarely ordered are kept at the bottom while the ones that are frequently ordered can be seen on the top.

- *Real-time decision making:* In logistics, there are a wide range of tasks that require data to make decisions. For example, finding the best possible route, scheduling, and choosing the most optimal carrier—all of these decisions will take a few minutes for the average human mind to compute. But with the help of BoIT, there is an instant solution for it as it sifts through thousands of data points. All of this takes only a few seconds and the accuracy is spot on.

Manufacturing

The application of BoIT for enhanced and efficient production and continuous maintenance is gaining traction as manufacturers realize the importance of AI in effective and timely identification and maintenance of the production line and the technology's role in reducing the downtime. A major share of expenses is accounted for by the continuous maintenance of production line equipment. This can weigh down heavily on the bottom line of asset-oriented production operation. Reports also indicate that manufacturers record annual unplanned downtime costs of U.S. $50 billion, with 42 percent of the unplanned downtime resulting from asset failure. Vendors too, like TIBCO, are providing the software platforms for connected intelligence that enables smart manufacturing as shown in Figure 4.5.

A few use cases:

- *BoIT's role in optimizing supply chain:* As mentioned before in logistics, BoIT can also enhance manufacturing supply chains. The AI algorithms can study consumer behavior, weather, socioeconomic and macroeconomic, political status,

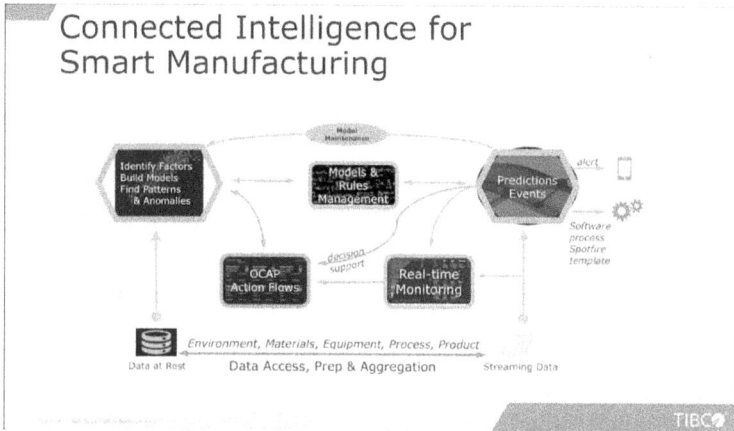

Figure 4.5 Connected intelligence in manufacturing

Source: TIBCO

and geographic patterns to formulate estimations for market demands. This information can help producers in predicting changes in the market and optimize energy consumption, inventory levels, supply of raw materials, and staffing to better respond to the market changes.

- *Generative design software:* BoIT is also capable of improving the way we design the products, as it can recommend solutions based on the detailed brief provided by the engineers and designers by way of generative design software (AI-powered software). The brief can include different parameters like available manufacturing methods and material types as well as restrictions like time and budget constraints. The software can process the detailed brief, explore different permutations and combinations, and recommend most optimum product options. The recommended solutions can then be tested for actual performance across different manufacturing conditions and scenarios for finding the best of all proposed solutions.

- *Predictive maintenance:* Both unplanned and planned downtimes can be easily tackled with the help of predictive maintenance, facilitated by BoIT. Predictive maintenance leverages AI's key components—artificial neural networks and machine learning—to formulate predictions related to asset malfunction. The AI algorithms continuously assess the production process and flag anomalies (even microscopic faults) in order to take timely maintenance and repair actions for reducing the risk of unplanned downtime. It can also help in prolonging the Remaining Useful Life (RUL) production machineries. The minute-by-minute update on production gathered and studied by the AI algorithms offers the technicians with insight into the components that need inspection in the cases where maintenance is necessary.

- *Quality of production:* With customers expecting faultless products and companies under constant pressure of very short time-to-market deadlines, offering a product with high quality that meets quality standards and regulations can give a manufacturer sleepless nights. Industry 4.0 has given way to the new Quality 4.0 model, under which traditional quality methods are combined with the new technologies like machine learning, Big Data, and AI among others to attain operational excellence. AI algorithms can alert the production teams about emerging faults like subtle abnormalities in the functioning of machines, deviations from recipes, and other such issues that can cause issues with product quality.

Just a number of examples where BoIT is heavily disrupting industries. Most likely, there are more that need investigation.

Chapter Takeaways

- This chapter explains the business value when converging blockchain, IoT, and data science/AI into the BoIT.
- The BoIT is turning a number of industries upside down including automotive, customer services, energy, health care, logistics and operations, and manufacturing.
- Statistics indicate that early adopters will be able to generate five times more revenue than late adopters.

Management Questions for Your Business

- How will you create a short list for suitable AI or ML applications?
- Describe each AI or ML application on your short list. Think of topics like application description, benefits and risks, security and budgets for hardware, software, and personnel. Forecast tangible and intangible results or savings.
- Totalize forecasted costs or budgets and forecasted results or savings of all AI or ML applications.
- Select the AI or ML application with the highest cash flow.

References and Additional Reading

Allen, P.R., and J.J. Bambara. 2020. *Blockchain, IoT, and Ai: Using the Power of Three to Develop Business, Technical, and Legal Solution.* New York, NY: McGraw-Hill Education.

Bacquet, J., and O. Vermesan. 2018. *Next Generation Internet of Things: Distributed Intelligence at the Edge and Human Machine-to-Machine Cooperation.* Gistrup, Denmark: River Publishers.

http://healthitanalytics.com/

http://internetofbusiness.com/

http://itweb.co.za/

http://simplilearn.com/

http://technologyreview.com/

http://towardsdatascience.com/

http://tractica.com/

CHAPTER 5

Required Skills, Jobs, and Future

Nowadays, everyone wants to optimize their businesses and their practices in an automated way to make their day-to-day living much better. Well, AI is a part of automation, and automation has become one of the sizzling topics nowadays due to probable jobs. It is expected that automation will eradicate 73 million more jobs by 2030, but in the field of AI, automation is producing jobs as well. Experts forecast that AI will provide jobs to 23 million candidates by the year 2020. Programming, testing, development, support, and maintenance are a few jobs that will be created in the field of AI. According to Indeed, the average salary for AI engineer ranges from approximately $75,835 per year for a research scientist to $144,468 per year for deep learning engineer.

Presently, the demand for blockchain technology is growing rapidly, and thus increases demand for the skillful experts. Well, blockchain-related jobs are the second-fastest enhancing job category with many job openings for blockchain developer. A blockchain developer mainly concentrates on creating and implementing architecture and solutions. The average salary of blockchain developer is approximately $158,000 in the United States. Also, the other job roles available in this field are software engineers, consultants, project managers, and so on.

Internet of Things (IoT) is a giant network of connected devices which collects and shares data about how they are used and about the environment in which they are operated. Security is a major concern these days, as everything which is connected to the Internet can be hacked easily. A report says that the need for securing every linked device is crucial and around 7.3 billion devices need to make secure before 2020. Thus, professionals with cyber-security specialized in IoT are in much demand. The average salary for IoT developers ranges from $59,849 to $123,163.

There's no single cause of the global technology skills gaps, and there is not one single point in time to trace its roots to. The simple truth is technology changes so fast and so dramatically that it's difficult to keep up. The main outcome of the global skills gap is disruption. If you don't overcome the skills gap, and your competitors do, you will be disrupted.

Technology makes education accessible to many, including those from various socioeconomic backgrounds and abilities. However, technology is not only changing the way we learn, but also the way education is taught by those in the field. Unsurprisingly for those interested in studying education, huge advancements in technology have made studying education a vastly different experience from students of yesteryear. This includes improving opportunities for communication and collaboration, among many other things.

New technology is changing the future of work with unprecedented speed and intensity, driving the reinvention of our lives and economy. Advances in robotics, AI, and machine learning push the frontier of what machines can do, making use of huge increases in ever-cheaper computing power and exponential growth in the data that's available to train them.

Obviously, technology relies heavily on people and their skills, as you can see in Figure 5.1.

Figure 5.1 Technology relies heavily on people

Source: LinkedIn Blogs

How to Solve the Digital Skills Gap?

The Widening Talent Gap

Here's a big problem looming on the horizon for the digital and tech sector. The struggle currently being experienced in finding talent has the potential of turning into a full-blown crisis in the next few years. According to a report "Future of Work—The Global Talent Crunch," the cost of labor shortage is expected to cost the U.S. technology, media, and tele-communications (TMT) sector $162.2 billion in unrealized output.

And the problem isn't limited to the United States. Every major player around the world, with the exception of India, is expected to have a shortage of skilled labor by 2030 totaling 4.3 million workers. The effects of the crisis have a potentially broader impact since technology touches all the other sectors in the economy. To compound the problem, the need for skilled technology labor will not be limited to the tech sector, as other industries will also be in need of this specialized workforce.

What Does It Take for Digital Transformation?

Having the right mix of skills within your organization will be critical for navigating your way through a digital transformation successfully. The required skills may vary throughout the process. As a leader, you need to be able to recruit a workforce with the right competencies at the right moment. You will also need to provide additional skills training to your current employees so that they can continue to meet your present needs and prepare for future business requirements.

Here are some of the top skills identified as crucial across industries:

- *AI and machine learning:* Systems can improve processes automatically through experience and without programming through machine learning. These types of programs, which are a form of AI, access and analyze data in order to learn from it.
- *Big Data analysis:* With the adoption of Big Data, businesses can gain an understanding of their customers' behavior now

and better predict future behavior and trends so that they can plan for them and start implementing the necessary changes.

- *Change management skills:* Digital transformation is a new kind of change management where companies are constantly seeking and exploring new digital strategies to implement. Your ability to recognize that change and to communicate it effectively will be a critical skill. Your teams may need to evolve and even be dispersed, so your communications and intercultural skills will be put to the test as you work to keep the spirit of teamwork thriving.
- *Cloud computing:* Without cloud computing, there can be no digital transformation. The dynamic and boundless resources made available by the cloud make a rapid business change not only possible but also far more viable. The more a business embraces a digital transformation philosophy, the more likely they are to gain the most benefit from their cloud solutions.
- *Cyber-security:* The protection of personal and confidential data must be of paramount importance to any enterprise. The trust of their customers and the success of future endeavors rely on the security, availability, and integrity of their data sources.
- *Enterprise mobility management: All* businesses recognize the critical role and the extent to which mobility is a valuable tool in digital transformation. However, few of them adequately take enterprise mobility management into account in their large-scale planning. Without a solid enterprise mobility management plan in place, businesses will have a hard time integrating mobile in their systems and leveraging its power.

The skills gap is high at the moment and will remain nearly as high in the future as you can see in Figure 5.2.

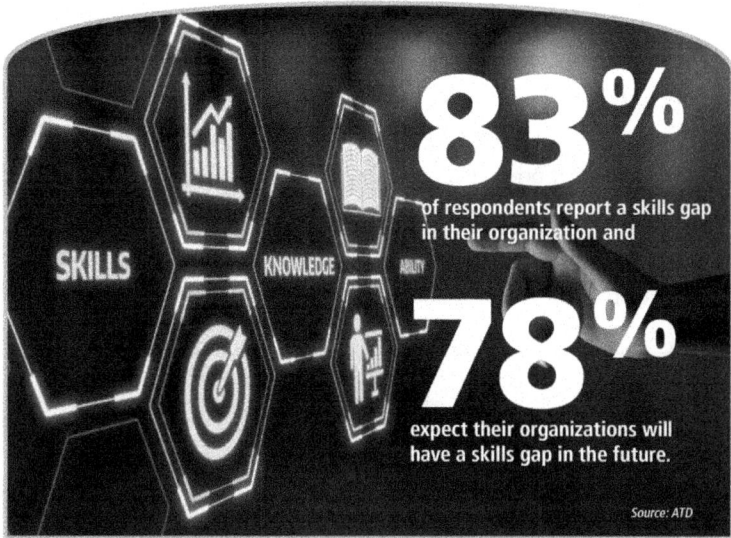

Figure 5.2 Skills gap now and in the future

Source: HRO Today

Soft Skills That Will Future-Proof Companies

Soft skills which are important in digital transformation are as follows:

- *Creative thinking:* Unforeseen problems will surely arise during the process, and to solve them, you will need creative minds. Creative people can often come up with innovative new ways of addressing an issue. Create an environment where any idea can come to the surface, no matter how unlikely or improbable it is. Creative thinkers aren't afraid to take risks and generate lots of ideas and put off analyzing how good those ideas are until later. Creative people are lateral thinkers who join two disparate concepts to form an idea or a solution.
- *Critical thinking:* After ideas have been generated, that's when it's time to call upon your faculties of critical thought to try to poke holes in the ideas. Critical thought is needed in the

analysis and synthesis of data in order to interpret and understand it using reason. It's the cornerstone to complex problem solving, deliberation, and decision making.

- *Emotional intelligence (EQ):* The ability to identify, understand, and moderate one's own emotions as well as those of others. It is becoming increasingly accepted that EQ is a leading factor in a person's success. Emotionally intelligent people tend to work better collaboratively, be better listeners, have fewer conflicts, and have a greater ability to communicate effectively. Since teamwork and the ability to communicate complex concepts to others are important in a digital transformation, it's easy to understand why having a high EQ is a significant asset.

- *Flexibility and determination:* In an essential period of transition, it probably seems quite obvious to say that flexibility is a necessary skill. The ability to adapt to new realities, to reorganize when things don't go according to plan, and to stay committed in the face of setbacks are qualities that you and your team members need.

Skill Acquisition or Talent Acquisition?

When it comes to filling skill gaps, the biggest challenge organizations face today is choosing between skill acquisition and talent acquisition. While recruiting and picking new candidates with the latest technology skills has its appeal, there are some significant benefits in upskilling your existing workforce—which also helps in employee retention, reputation, and profitability of the company.

The Solution

Organizations across the globe are realizing the possibility of fulfilling their hiring needs with talent from within the organization. However, a pure-play upskilling strategy might mean missing out on engaging with game changing talent in the industry. The answer is to adopt a healthy mix of skill acquisition and talent acquisition. The core of any company is built on a solid policy of hiring the best talent in the market, but once they're in place, it's important to continually upskill that new talent with the latest tools and technologies in the market. These include such skills as digital marketing, cloud computing, Big Data and analytics, and cyber-security. Branching off from this further, skill acquisition by itself presents its own set of unique challenges. Here are the pressing ones:

Scalability and Sustainability

The primary problem of introducing any form of employee training is affordability. On top of that, if the job market favors employees, with a high demand for the skills they have or acquire, there is the risk that they may take those skills elsewhere, and new employees will have to be trained. How do you ensure gradual upskilling of your employees, with emphasis on long-term relevance and retention of these skilled personnel within your organization?

The Solution

Segregating employees into well-defined categories helps you identify the precise, relevant training that is likely to be beneficial, rather than inconveniently signing up all your employees to all of the training sessions. This requires and demonstrates a high degree of empathy and nuanced ability to assess the needs of your employees. Investing in virtual or online training is a cost-effective solution, which also comes with the advantage of empowering your employees to pick and juggle their hours, ensuring it doesn't affect their productivity during work hours.

This approach also makes sure your employees end up acquiring skills that will directly provide them a career boost and a step-up in roles and responsibilities, criteria very integral to preserving job satisfaction.

Keeping Employees Motivated

The average employee has enough mission-critical work to do to keep going from 9 to 5 every day of the week and beyond. That leaves little time for training. Expecting eagerness and enthusiasm to learn and develop more skills on top of that requires a certain degree of additional persuasion.

The Solution

- *Make learning interesting, not intimidating:* Although the easiest way to take this up would be to generate a sense of fear and job insecurity among employees by making training mandatory, such negative incentivizing actually creates stress and dread of training, which inhibits learning and retention. Instead, motivate your employees first by telling them the reasons why additional learning is needed for them as individuals as well as the entire organization. Also, make the training fun and easy to access. You can make the training even more interesting by including gamification elements.
- *Provide managerial visibility and support:* Integrating a Learning Management System (LMS) into your corporate training programs gives managers visibility into the team's ongoing progress. This continuous oversight allows managers to step in and offer encouragement or help when they see someone falling behind.
- *Encourage competition and social support:* Using a leaderboard or posting employee progress creates a sense of mutual participation as well as competitiveness that can drive many employees to complete training and achieve certifications faster.

Resistant Learners

The cream always rises to the top, and true to this logic, the top layer of talent in your organization will always find training useful, take courses, and pick up new skills. The ones who resist this will need convincing and incentivizing in order to fall into the reskill cycle.

The Solution

To prevent lack of course engagement and a "going through the motions" routine from interfering with actual skill acquisition, here are some methods to improve training effectiveness, even with reluctant or slow learners:

- *Adjacent training:* This method insists on teaching new skills that are similar and closely related to the employee's existing domain of expertise, making it a more straightforward process for them to pick up the skill without any stress or unjustified effort. In the long run, this translates to employees gradually consuming the entire array of skills.
- *Feature expert trainers:* Courses and webinars hosted by industry experts have a positive effect on the learner, who is motivated to work harder and validate the learnings from an actual domain authority.
- *Structured, chunked learning:* To provide a more engaging experience, the learners must be able to follow a well-charted, structured path that they can follow. Divide your courses into smaller, easy-to-digest sections.

An active emphasis on innovative skill acquisition strategies complemented by talent acquisition when necessary creates the optimal way for an organization to achieve its goals and realize the fine lines between holistic progress and the collapsible tipping point. Such an approach also encourages a mutually beneficial model, boosting the growth of both the organization and the individual.

Future of Work

Imagine your workplace 10 years from now. Chances are it'll be very different from today thanks to fast-evolving technologies that are changing the nature of work, the dynamics of the workforce, and the notion of the workplace.

Figure 5.3 Future of work—humans and robots

Source: Financial Times

To stay relevant and competitive, you need to understand the impact of emerging technologies on the future of work. You must incorporate these innovations strategically to attract the right talent, increase efficiencies, and improve the bottom line.

The common scenario says that the future workforce will consist of humans who will be working with robots. This is visualized in Figure 5.3. Another scenario says that robots will overtake the world. It will probably take a decade to find out what the scenario will be.

How the Future of Work Will Change

Emerging technologies will impact the future of work in these major categories:

- *How work is done*: Advances in AI-driven technologies and robotics will increase the range and amount of work that can be done by smart machines. Within the next 15 years, 38 percent of U.S. jobs will likely be automated, affecting at least 100 million knowledge workers by 2025. Meanwhile, jobs will become less routine, and roles will be redefined by connecting technology with human skills and advanced expertise. Organizations will need to innovate how humans work alongside machines.

- *The nature of work*: Technologies will minimize the need to perform repetitive tasks manually. While fewer workers will be hired for manual tasks, more will be employed for job functions that involve creative and strategic thinking. The nature of work will shift from focusing on task completion. Problem solving, communication, listening, interpretation, and design will gain prominence. The ability to learn new skills will be more valuable than having specific knowledge. Organizations will seek out workers that have the mental ductility to learn continuously.

- *Where the work is done*: New communication platforms break down barriers among multiple office locations and remote teams to enable seamless collaboration. Organizations can transcend the limitations of distance and tap into a global talent pool so tasks can be completed as cost-effectively as possible. However, the distributed model requires companies to rethink how they can foster culture and team connections within a virtual working environment to nurture and retain increasingly scarce talent.

- *Who does the work*: Technology allows organizations to leverage a continuum of full-time employees and freelancers to managed services and gig workers in the most cost-efficient way. Companies will reconsider the employee life cycle. They'll use multiple employment formats to obtain the creativity, passion, experience, expertise, and skill sets needed for the project at hand. As such, hiring will focus on problem-solving ability and task performance rather than filling roles in the organization chart.

Key Emerging Technologies That Will Reshape the Future of Work

The notion of work is fast evolving, and here are the key emerging technologies that impact the future of work:

- *AI-driven technologies*: The AI umbrella encompasses machine learning, deep learning, natural language processing, natural language generation, and more. The use of AI allows organizations to efficiently extract insights from their proprietary business data for accurate and timely decision making. Of course, organizations must first embrace automation to generate this business data. Meanwhile, the reduction of repetitive tasks allows employees to focus on strategic and creative work that's more valuable and meaningful. AI is making work more enjoyable and fulfilling by augmenting the capabilities of knowledge workers. AI' s ability to process large amounts of data and extract insights helps humans cut through the clutter and figure out where to focus their attention to enhance strategic thinking and decision making.
- *Cloud-based communication platforms*: Unified communications (UC) platforms enable organizations to leverage the benefits of a remote workforce effectively. These cloud-based technologies help streamline workflow, facilitate collaboration, and increase efficiencies. They enable real-time communication and collaboration through functionalities such as voice and video calls, instant messaging, and screen and file sharing. They allow companies to access a global workforce and attract talent without being hindered by inefficient communications. A UC platform is the hub of a digital workplace. It introduces a global element to many workforces.
- *Digital talent platforms*: The ability to access talent from all over the world through a variety of work arrangements is promoting organizations to reconsider their talent model and employee life cycle. The use of digital talent platforms reduces the impact of a mismatch between skills, availability, and location. Companies will shift from filling specific roles to hiring talent based on the skills required to complete a specific project successfully. With technologies and business requirements always in flux, specific skills will matter less. The ability to obtain new knowledge and adapt to new technological solutions will become the key to success.

- *Visual, low-code process automation*: Automation is key to increasing efficiency, reducing human error, and lowering operational costs. Fewer workers will be needed for repetitive tasks, and more employees will focus on strategic decision making and creative problem solving. There are two main types of process automation technologies: Robotic Process Automation (RPA) and Business Process Automation (also called Business Process Management or BPM). RPA automates individual tasks that are repetitive and time-consuming with very little added value. It cuts cost without the need to change the underlying infrastructure. BPM is the automation of end-to-end business processes and often serves as the strategic foundation of an organization's digital transformation

Future of Education

The way Industry 4.0 is transforming the world, technologies like IoT, Big Data, and AI are impacting major industries, and in turn, jobs. This implies that Industry 4.0 will not only affect industries but consequently transform the way jobs and education will be seen. This will result in the Future of Education, also known as Education 4.0.

It can be said that Industry 4.0 will affect the roles for which today's students will be prepared. This will require educational institutions to produce a workforce for working in this technologically transformed era. Further, it will also require the current workforce to upgrade their skills and knowledge to match these newly created job roles. For this, a revolution in education is essential to enable people worldwide to harness the opportunities created by the advent of these technologies.

This transformation of the education industry will make it more personalized, peer-to-peer, and a continuous process. So, what is Education 4.0? Let's look at some pointers that can describe the Future of Education:

- It will cater to the need of Industry 4.0 enabling the workforce and machines to align to explore new possibilities.
- It will create a blueprint for the future of learning—from school-based learning to learning at the workplace.

- It will deploy the potential of digital technologies, open-sourced content, and personalized data of this globally connected and tech-driven world.

Figure 5.4 shows a classroom with students who may have their own learning program because they use virtual and augmented reality. This way each student can follow their own course in their own tempo.

A few trends in Education 4.0 are as follows:

- *Accelerate remote learning:* Education 4.0 will enable learning anytime, anywhere as the e-learning tools and applications will provide opportunities for remote, self-paced learning. The role of classrooms will change wherein theoretical knowledge will be imparted outside the classroom while practical or experiential knowledge will be imparted face to face.
- *Changes in exam pattern and assessment:* Here, it is essential to understand that a traditional Q&A or subjective writing examination may not suffice the needs of future talent requirements. This means that the assessments, as part of Education 4.0, will not be solely based on the current exam-

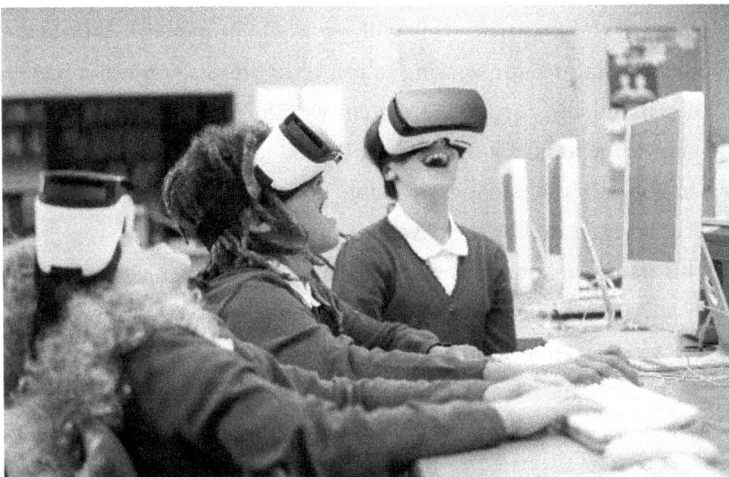

Figure 5.4 Future of digital education

Source: Future Agenda

ination patterns. It will be done by analyzing their learning journey through practical and experiential learning-based projects or field works.

- *Choice of education tools:* A part of Education 4.0 will be the technology/devices used by students to gain an education. While every subject has its own set of knowledge and information, the road to attaining this knowledge can vary. This means that the students will be able to choose the tools and techniques through which they want to acquire this knowledge. Blended learning and BYOD (Bring Your Own Device) are a few examples of this.

- *Data analysis:* There were times when analysts used to collect and sort data manually—now done through computers. Additionally, computers will also be used for all kinds of statistical analysis—describing and analyzing data and predicting future trends. Education 4.0 will train students to apply theoretical knowledge and use human reasoning to examine the patterns and predict trends.

- *Field-specific experience:* As technology integration facilitates more efficiency, the education curriculum will now accommodate more skills that require human knowledge and personal interaction. This means that schools will now provide more opportunities for students to obtain real-world skills that are relevant to the prospecting job opportunities.

- *Personalized learning:* Education 4.0 will also enable personalized learning for students depending on their capabilities. This means that above-average students will be challenged with tasks that are difficult as compared to students who are below average. This implies that there will be individual learning processes for each student. It will surely have a positive impact as it will enable students to learn at their pace. This will result in a better understanding of the concepts and an overall better result.

- *Project-based learning:* The freelance economy is on the rise and will continue to do so. This means that the students of today will need to adapt to project-based learning and working styles. They will need to hone their skills and learn how to apply and mold them as per situations. This part of Education 4.0 will teach them organizational skills, time management skills, and collaborative skills that they can further use in their academic careers as well as employment.

The impact of technology on the education industry will not only transform the way it is imparted, but also the way students perceive education. Education 4.0 or the Future of Education will change the teaching–learning methodologies to make the students future-ready. It is time to witness this change so that we can move toward a progressive, intellectual, knowledge-driven, and future-ready world.

Chapter Takeaways

- Experts forecast that technologies such as blockchain, IoT, and AI will provide jobs to many million candidates, although more people will lose their jobs.
- Statistics indicate that early adopters will be able to generate five times more revenue than late adopters.
- Overview of the top skills identified as crucial across industries and soft skills that will future-proof companies.
- Choosing between skill acquisition and talent acquisition.
- The impact of emerging technologies on the future of work.
- The transformation of the education industry to a more personalized, peer-to-peer, and a continuous process resulting in Education 4.0.

Management Questions for Your Business

- How do you create a list of required skills and functions in blockchain, IoT, and AI?
- How do you describe each skill or function including job description, required education, internal or external experts?
- What are the total forecasted costs or budgets and forecasted results or savings of each skill and function?
- What are the skills and functions with the highest priority?

References and Additional Reading

Calle, H., R. Talwar, S. Wells, and A. Whittington. 2018. *A Very Human Future: Enriching Humanity in a Digitized World*. Tonbridge, UK: Fast Future Publishing.

http://digitalmarketinginstitute.com/

http://elearningindustry.com/

http://futurereadyedu.com/

http://simplilearn.com/

http://techdeeps.com/

http://weforum.org/

http://zarantech.com/

CHAPTER 6

Industrial IoT (IIoT) Platforms

There are many vendors in the IIoT platform marketplace, offering remarkably similar capabilities and methods of deployment. And not one of them has differentiated itself enough at this point to be a clear leader in an emerging market. Gartner's June 2019 Magic Quadrant for Industrial IoT Platforms, for example, has no leaders or challengers. Have a glance at Figure 6.1 to see Gartner's Magic Quadrant for Industrial IoT Platforms.

Given the fractured and crowded market, and the growing potential of IIoT to extract value from data, reduce costs, improve operations, and present new business models, analysts recommend that businesses looking for a platform devote time to research. They also suggest focusing on industry-specific use cases and outcomes.

Prime use cases in manufacturing are production monitoring and inventory management. In oil and gas, the use cases are supply chain optimization and worker safety. And many IIoT use cases relate to core overall operational efficiency, equipment monitoring, and predictive maintenance because any downtime is extremely costly.

Simply put, IIoT platforms create a vital, single view of an operation. Their function is a "superset" of an IoT platform in that it shares common core functions. According to industry analysts, the most important functionality an IIoT platform should provide are:

- **Device management** software that connects thousands to hundreds of thousands of sensors, industrial machines, and digital systems. IIoT solutions are usually designed to identify failures and facilitate recovery from failure.

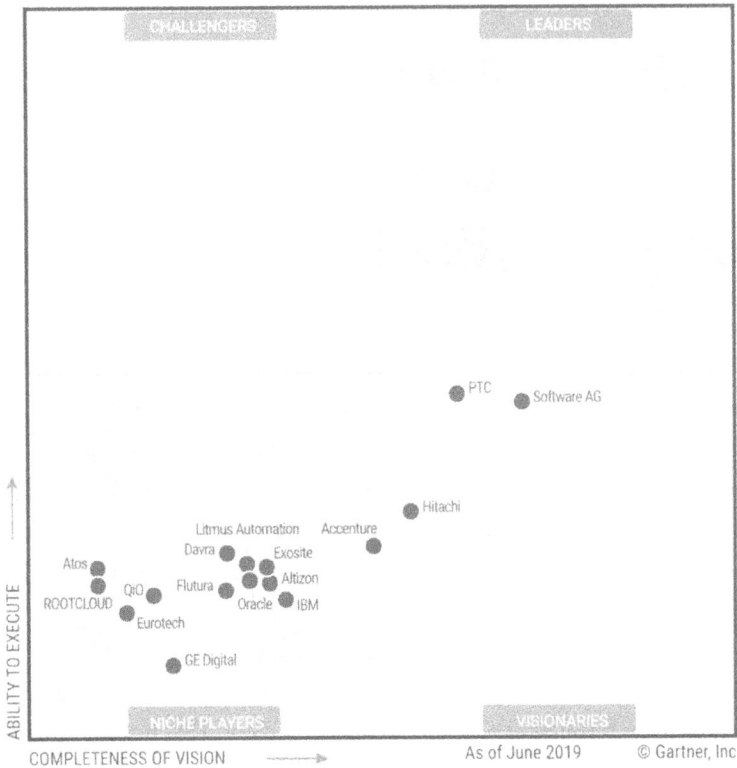

Figure 6.1 Top IIoT platforms

Source: Gartner

- **Integration** through software development kits, development tools, and APIs to support business processes and enterprise systems across the business. There are significant challenges, however, given the array of back-office applications such as ERP, application performance management, enterprise asset management, computerized maintenance management systems, and more.
- **Data management** to control and monitor ingestion, storage, accessibility, flow.
- **Analytics** of data from connected devices, the enterprise, and third parties to reveal patterns and optimization of assets.

An IIoT platform should also be able to orchestrate functions such as machine learning (ML), using edge computing, as the volume of time-series data in some forms of manufacturing is too great to transfer to the cloud. Also, the latency required to act upon the data such as in safety or critical situations is too long in the cloud.

Another challenge to full-cloud deployment comes from the industrial organizations themselves and the culture of engineers that "places high trust in what they can touch and control," according to Gartner, which expects that 30 percent of industrial enterprises will have full, on-premises deployments of IIoT platforms in 2023, up from 15 percent this year.

What Is an IIoT Platform?

An IIoT platform is a modular software system that helps connect a diverse set of equipment ("things"), manages the data flow, provides data analytics abilities, and supports application development to make sense and use of the processed data.

IoT Solution Architecture

A typical solution architecture consists of four key components:

1. *Business applications/integrations:* A library of backend IT system integrators to ensure machine data is fed into key IT systems to complete the circle of operations. Integrations to key systems such as ERP, BI, QMS, and planning, and scheduling are super important. Plus, the platform should provide a range of business (sector-specific) applications or the ability to build such applications to cater to specific verticals.

2. *Intelligent edge gateway:* This is a software component close to things, which is capable of collecting, aggregating, sanitizing stream of light data, and push an aggregate/relevant result to the IoT cloud. This acts as a mediator between the things and the cloud IoT platform.

3. *IoT cloud:* This is a core IoT platform capable of handling massive amounts of data with data analytics, ML, and AI capabilities. Its core capabilities include, but are not limited to, device management and stream analytics including complex events processing, rules engine,

alerts and notifications, Big Data, and ML capabilities, and other vital platform services such as authentication, multitenancy, end-to-end security, scheduling engine, SDKs, and platform APIs.

4. *Things:* These are the actual machines or systems which are monitored by collecting their data. This is the source of your data.

How to Select an IIoT Platform

Key Factors to Consider While Choosing Your IIoT Platform

- *Deployment flexibility:* Different organizations have different needs, technology maturity, and internal capabilities to support third-party software. An organization may demand fully on-premise deployment to keep entire control with them or may choose to go with private or public cloud-based option to achieve higher efficiency and cost savings. Sometimes, you may begin with on-premise deployment and graduate into a cloud-based model. Whatever may be the case, your platform must be flexible in providing different deployment options.

- *Ease of use:* If the systems are complicated, the adoption suffers. Your IoT platform must be easy to learn, adapt, and operate. The lesser the roadblocks, the better the adoption. Your IoT platform will be used by your shop floor people, management team, your IT maintenance engineers, your suppliers/vendors, and, in some cases, even your customers or your partners, too. Hence, it's super important to have an easy learning curve and an easy-to-maintain IoT platform.

- *Interoperability:* Your organization data resides in multiple systems and in a variety of formats. The IoT platform should be capable to integrate with your backend IT systems such as ERP, CRM, QMS, planning, and scheduling. This makes your IoT project successful, as such integrations help feed real-time relevant machine data into critical IT systems to help make data-driven decisions.

- *Proof of validations:* Lastly, you don't want to be a guinea pig for a risky project. Ensure that the IoT platform has sufficient community of customers and developers. You should request for customer references and check how they are benefited with the platform in use. A good partner and developer ecosystem is a sign of good global support. Both partners and developer ecosystem can help deploy and configure faster and achieve time to market. Certificates of third-party validations such as security or platform stability or customer testimonials may be a good filtration criterion to choose a platform.

- *Security and scalability:* Your data is your key asset. Hence, data security is of prime importance. IoT is still at a relatively early stage and yet to mature in its security framework. It's imperative that your cloud IoT platform offers comprehensive security majors at things level, while data in flight and data at rest. Next, your IoT platform must have an enterprise-grade performance guarantee. Your IoT projects may begin with a small pilot, but IoT initiatives are mostly part of digital transformation projects across the enterprise. Hence, while choosing the IoT platform, you have to see into the future to define scalability requirements.

- *Support for connectivity protocols:* Every IoT project has several components as mentioned in IoT solution architecture. Things, hardware, sensors, OT systems, and edge gateway are elements that come into the picture even before the data reaches the IoT cloud. In the majority of IoT projects, the biggest challenge is to connect the machines to collect the data. There is a wide range of communication protocols that your platform edge need to support. Ethernet, OPC—UA/DA, CSV/XML, just to name a few, are widely used protocols that any IoT platform must support.

- *Understand your needs:* Without getting driven by the hype or management pressure, a first important aspect is to under-stand why you need IoT and what do you intend to achieve with IoT. A lot of people have a question when I have auto-mation in place, why I need IoT, or the misconception that

> IoT will replace all my SCADA, DCS, and ERP systems. Key
> benefits of IoT are when you tap into the power of data ana-
> lytics and are able to connect your IT and OT systems across
> the plant or multiple plants. You need to look at IoT as a big
> picture rather than a point solution to fix a small problem.

There are hundreds of IoT platforms. Choosing from a long list of platforms could be a daunting task. Leading technology analyst firms such
as Gartner, Forrester, and IDC have published their study of various IoT
platforms with detailed evaluation criteria. You may refer to some of these
reports to narrow your focus and get closure on a confident decision.

The IIoT Platform Market

Owing to its extensive application and adoption in an enormous range
of industries including energy and utilities, chemicals and materials, food
and beverage, water and waste management, automotive, machine manufacturing, semiconductor and electronics, medical devices, and logistics
and transportation, the IIoT platform marketplace is poised for exponential growth as it grips these verticals as an inevitable adoption. The staggering growth of the IoT market—see Figure 6.2—has caused so many
IIoT platforms to be developed.

With a huge number of economies dependent on oil and gas as their
principal source of energy, this arcade is witnessing rampage production
demand. To counter this unprecedented demand, oil and gas sector is
heavily adopting IIoT platforms to converge its operations with economic efficiency. Owing to such intense rate of application, the oil and
gas sector currently dominates the application segment of the global IIoT
platforms market, with the demand incrementing at a CAGR of 12.1
percent going through 2024. Warning from the World Bank in its latest report regarding more heightened volatility in oil markets in 2019
because of unusual spare production capacity among OPEC members has
installed a demand for IIoT in oil and gas sector for economical production. IIoT platforms loaded with low-cost sensors, IoT cloud platforms,
IoT device management platform, application management platform,
and connectivity management platform enable predictive maintenance,

The Industrial IoT (IIoT) Market Map

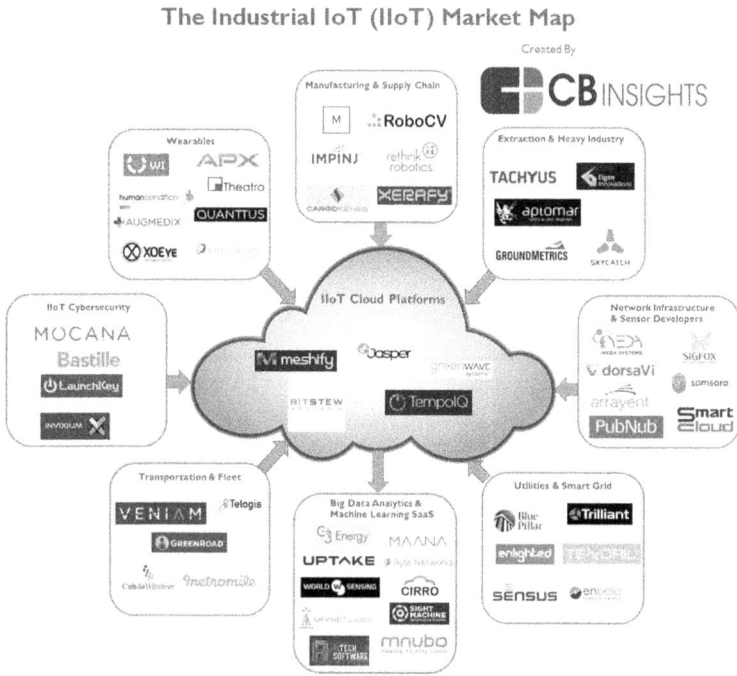

Figure 6.2 IIoT market map

Source: IoT Central

improve process flow achieved by monitoring changes in operating conditions, increase productivity, and reduce accident frequency with real-time monitoring of assets.

SELECT USA, a federal organization of the Unites States to promote foreign direct investment, figured out that the logistics and transportation industry in the United States generates revenue close to 7.5 percent of the annual U.S. GDP bringing the amount close to $1.4 trillion. IIoT platform market solutions merging with transportation is evolving this sector in an exceptional manner:

- It empowers road, rail, air, and shipping manufacturers and marine managing enterprises to connect with their technicians anytime, anywhere, allowing them to be vigilant with in-field repairs and maintenance.

- IIoT platform market companies are providing improved user experience to customers using mobile devices and improved diagnostics to their service personnel.
- Improved diagnostics: Connectivity between diagnostic PC applications and native vehicle networks assists service personnel and dealers to easily repair key functioning apparatuses on the vehicle.

All these efficient and economic operational traits have diverted the global existing transportation arcade toward installation of IIoT, thus pushing this application industry segment to grow at a staggering CAGR of 31.3 percent through 2025.

As per an acute regional outlook analysis of global IIoT platform market, North America dominates with 33.5 percent of global market size under its own territory as of 2018. Apart from the aforementioned oil and gas and transportation industry, this region is witnessing application of IIoT in its flourishing medical devices arcade, F&B consumption and its logistics, and water and waste management facilities as a consequence of industrialization and energy and utilities sector feeding the perpetual urban population needs.

Global IIoT Platform Vendors

Some of the key players on the IIoT platform market are G.E. (Predix), Siemens (Mindsphere), Hitachi (Vantara), Honeywell (Uniformance), ABB (Ability), IBM (Bluemix), Microsoft (Azure), Schneider (Wonderware), Atos (Codex), PTC (ThingWorx), C3 (C3IOT), SAP (HANA), Software AG (Cumulocity), Bosch (IoT Suite), and Cisco (Jasper).

ABB, a power and robotics company, is applying connected sensors to monitor the preservation necessities of its robots to volunteer repairs before parts break. KIST Europe and IBM are associates in SmartFactory-KL, a pioneering industrial facility constructed with integrated mechanisms that can be reconfigured for various manufacturing tasks. All the apparatus are instrumented with sensors and linked through the Internet of Things (IoT), to a comprehensive digital imitation of the factory's physical properties, procedures, and systems, running in the IBM Cloud.

As per the United Nations report, the number of networked devices (the "Internet of Things") will outnumber people by six to one by 2022. Similarly, a good chunk of recognized enterprises and industries have policies to implement digital-first business strategy (e.g., KIST Europe and IBM). So the existing setting already depicts that the IoT has already started enjoying a firm grip over personal consumers as well as industrial sphere. The unsaturated IIoT platform market displays all the potential and required caliber to replace daily assessment-management traditional equipment with IoT.

IIoT Platforms

Analyst house Gartner has put the leading IIoT platforms through their paces, and named the best in the business. Here, Enterprise IoT Insights reviews the Gartner review, and orders the results, to summarize the best IIoT platforms available to enterprises in the energy and utilities, manufacturing, and transportation and logistics sectors.

Accenture

- *Platform:* Communications Platform-as-a-Service (CPaaS)
- *Launch:* 2015
- *Industries:* energy and utilities, manufacturing, transportation and logistics
- *Use cases:* asset monitoring and predictive maintenance
- *Cloud:* private (on-premises), hybrid (IaaS), public (AWS/ Microsoft Azure)

Figure 6.3 refers to the introduction of CPaaS.

The pressure CIOs find themselves under is only likely to increase as customers become more and more demanding. This is why a platform approach to customer experience—namely, CPaaS—is growing in popularity among CIOs. In fact, IDC estimates that the CPaaS market will be worth $10.9 billion by 2022.

CPaaS sits across the company's various legacy systems, augmenting them by acting as a bridge between them and customer communications

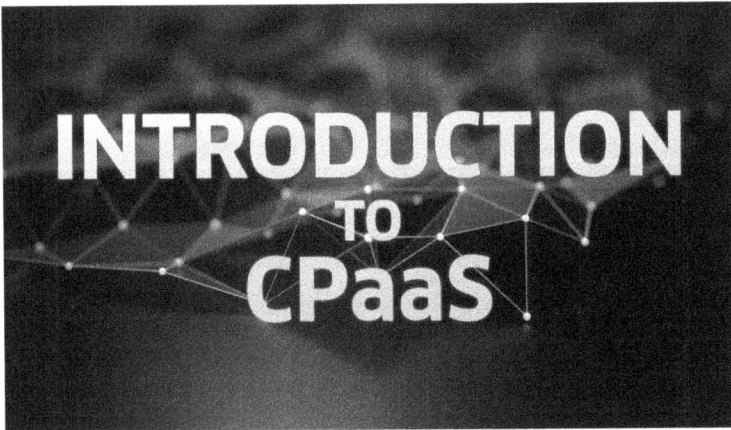

Figure 6.3 Introduction to CPaaS

Source: Alcatel Lucent

channels. This removes the need to "rip-and-replace" legacy IT systems at great expense and ensures that they can still deliver value without holding back agility. A central communications platform can also support the creation and management of multiple customer journeys. Using low-code development, visual composition, and "drag-and-drop" functionality, communications platforms allow companies to build, change, and optimize customer journeys in real time. A low-code approach also democratizes development, lessening the burden on IT and at the same time significantly reducing development processes and costs.

From an automation perspective, a platform approach makes it seamless to integrate and orchestrate customer interactions using NLP and AI. They provide the tools to launch, iterate, and orchestrate outbound one-way communications and interactive two-way communications, as well as multistep interactive customer journeys across any digital communications channel. This enables companies to increase operational efficiency and improve customer experience through automating channel-agnostic customer journeys, faster than was ever possible before.

Altizon

- *Platform:* Datonis
- *Launch:* n/a
- *Industries:* energy and utilities, manufacturing, transportation and logistics
- *Use cases:* real-time monitoring of assets for predictive failure and spares management
- *Cloud:* private (on-premises), hybrid (IaaS), public (AWS/ Microsoft Azure)

Datonis is a highly scalable, cloud-based IIoT platform for Industry 4.0, developed by Palo Alto-based company Altizon Systems that has been helping enterprises find their way through their IIoT transformation journey for the past six years. As a company that has been recognized for the second consecutive year in the Gartner 2019 Magic Quadrant for IIoT Platforms, Altizon has connected over 100 manufacturing plants with a list of implemented initiatives that continue to grow.

Their studies have shown them that every industry vertical has a unique set of obstacles or use cases best suited for IIoT while their focus has taught them that they can achieve faster ROI for their customers with a holistic approach. Datonis helps businesses realize measurable business results in areas such as energy efficiency, process quality improvement, and improved overall equipment effectiveness (OEE) for edge machines.

Datonis is a cloud-based IIoT platform that connects machines, people, and processes to drive digital transformation, utilizing machine data, analytics, and AI to drive outcomes. The platform is scalable and allows devices to:

- Connect and transfer data in real time, securely
- Analyze machine data in real time
- Set alerts and notifications for faults or errors
- Interactively analyze machine data at scale
- Use ML to build data models on the machine data and predict outcomes

- Consolidate the machine data with enterprise systems using
an open API

Now businesses can interactively analyze their machine data at scale and leverage the power of ML to build data models to predict outcomes.

Atos

- *Platform*: Codex IoT
- *Launch*: June 2016
- *Industries*: energy and utilities, manufacturing, transportation and logistics
- *Use cases:* include asset monitoring, quality, and predictive maintenance
- *Cloud:* private (on-premises), public (AWS/Microsoft Azure)

Atos offers Codex IoT, a set of IoT applications, blueprints, platforms, and business services, as well as development, hosting, and integration services on both its own and its partner's platforms, especially Siemens MindSphere. Atos provides a broad range of managed services for edge solutions; hybrid platforms; and, together with Worldline (its subsidiary specializing in payments and transaction services), IoT connectivity. The firm's customers are concentrated in Europe. However, in October 2018, the company merged with Syntel, expanding its North American presence; consultant resources; and vertical expertise, primarily in banking, finance, and insurance. (This acquisition occurred after the cutoff date for this analysis and thus is not reflected in Atos' score.)

Atos has a rich partner ecosystem and a willingness to collaborate with other vendors, which customers highlight as a key differentiator. It should continue to extend its partner ecosystem and innovation center presence to align with evolving IoT market requirements. Atos' road map focuses on blockchain, cognitive learning, AI, and ML, and multiplatform integration solutions to help firms manage the growing volume and complexity of IoT data. Enterprises turn to Atos for vertical solutions to address connected vehicles, connected homes, IIoT, smart grids, and energy and utilities markets.

Hitachi

- *Platform:* Lumada
- *Launch:* May 2016
- *Industries:* energy and utilities, manufacturing, transportation and logistics, natural resources
- *Use cases:* asset management, predictive maintenance, operational excellence
- *Cloud:* private (on-premises), hybrid (IaaS), public (AWS/Google/Microsoft Azure)

Figure 6.4 shows the data collection functionality of various data sources such as machine, human, and business data on the Lumada platform.

In general, Hitachi's Lumada IoT platform business is helping Hitachi coordinate its hundreds of businesses, which, incidentally, the conglomerate plans on thinning to roughly 500 entities by March 2022, according to Nikkei Asian Review.

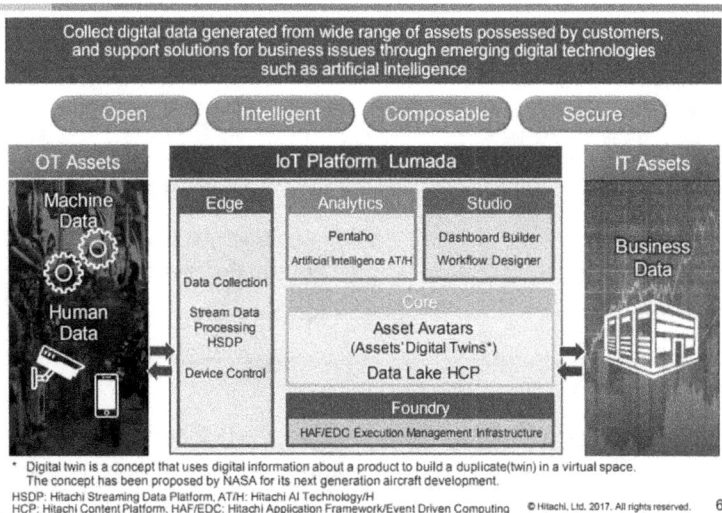

Figure 6.4 IIoT platform Lumada

Source: IoT Revolution

"Lumada is enabling us to standardize in terms of how we do IoT, and how we do data-driven solutions in the general sense," said Bjorn Andersson, senior director, global IoT marketing at Hitachi Vantara. "That's where Lumada came from." That is, Lumada was a mechanism to help the conglomerate standardize technologies and identify best practices it could extend across its operations "so we don't reinvent the wheel all over again, every time," Andersson added. Describing Lumada as "more than a platform," Andersson said the software is not limited to facilitating connectivity, data management, and security. It helps Hitachi Vantara customers meet business objectives, he said. "We're trying to build in domain expertise we have from all of these business areas, and manufacturing is a big one," Andersson said.

With Lumada Manufacturing Insights, however, Hitachi Vantara is not just leveraging its own internal manufacturing experience. "We are doing a lot of co-creation," Andersson said. And what it learns from that experience, it seeks to build into "more packaged solutions for our customers," he added. It is difficult to pinpoint the genesis of Lumada, but the company formally unveiled it to the public in 2016. The platform has been competitive in various IoT and IIoT rankings from the likes of Gartner, Forrester, and IDC in recent years.

IBM

- *Platform:* Watson IoT
- *Launch:* October 2014
- *Industries:* energy and utilities, insurance, manufacturing, retail
- *Use cases:* asset monitoring, predictive maintenance
- *Cloud:* private cloud (on-premises; isolated and single tenant), public cloud (multitenant)

The Watson IoT makes use of millions of sensors that work consistently and continuously to deliver a large amount of data for the effective performance of businesses. It has been possible to make the IoT a reality by making several technologies to come together that includes the Internet, microelectrical systems, and wireless communications to name a few. Ranging from digital twins to connected cars, the IoT has made our life unbelievably easy.

With almost everything ranging from cars to conveyor belts connected to the network, IoT has changed the working of every business. IBM Watson IoT offers a flexible, versatile, and scalable toolkit including gateway and application access for collecting the data of the connected device and analyzing it for growth. By making the use of Watson IoT, it has become possible for businesses to extract the connected device's data and valuable insights to enhance and improve the working of the business.

IBM has successfully identified the various IoT zones which hold a great potential to change the world which we live in with the potential benefits of IoT. IBM has also collaborated with many financial companies to offer a better and secured way and modes of payments. IBM has always been at its best in extending all the possible support to take the technology of IoT on a different level so that the world we are living in can turn to be more secure and comfortable.

Oracle

- *Platform:* Oracle IoT Cloud Service
- *Launch:* December 2015
- *Industries:* energy and utilities, manufacturing, transportation and logistics
- *Application focus:* asset monitoring, production monitoring, fleet monitoring
- *Cloud:* private (Oracle Cloud; available on-premise)

Oracle is a global software corporation known for its advanced database management. Its product line goes beyond cloud computing and enterprise software, offering an extensive IoT toolkit.

The Oracle IoT platform connects enterprise software with the *real world* of gadgets and their metrics. Oracle offers exceptional business-oriented opportunities through a user-friendly environment for building commercial apps. As a recognized leader in database management, Oracle can handle large amounts of data. For this reason, creating large-scale IoT ecosystems is not a problem at all.

In the age of data breaches, and security loopholes found literally everywhere, the use of advanced protection mechanisms is more than a good idea. It's no news that IoT ecosystems usually integrate with various devices. Since not all of them have security features already built in, it is essential to use centralized protection tools. Oracle takes advantage of high-quality security mechanisms. Reliable protection of IoT systems from any external threats is what makes Oracle exclusive.

The Oracle main goal is to help your products reach the market as soon as possible, using high-speed messaging and endpoint management, extending and improving your supply chain, customer experience apps, and operational efficiency. By using Oracle IoT cloud platform, you can connect your devices to the cloud, perform a real-time analysis research, and integrate acquired data with the company's apps or web services.

PTC

- *Platform:* ThingWorx
- *Launch:* January 2014 (acquired)
- *Industries:* energy and utilities, manufacturing, transportation and logistics
- *Use cases:* asset monitoring, predictive maintenance, operational excellence
- *Cloud:* private (on-premises), hybrid (IaaS), public (AWS/ Google/Microsoft Azure)

Figure 6.5 gives an overview of the PTC ThingWorx partner ecosystem, including large systems integrators such as CSC (Computer Science Corporation).

PTC ThingWorx is an application development platform for the IoT. PTC, a maker of computer-aided design (CAD) software and other tools manufacturers use to design, produce, and service their products, acquired ThingWorx in December 2013.

The PTC ThingWorx platform consists of five main components.

THINGWORX READY

THINGWORX POWERED

ThingWorx

THINGWORX VAR & INTEGRATOR

ThingWorx
Partner Ecosystem

Figure 6.5 PTC ThingWorx 7

Source: Internet of Business

1. *ThingWorx Foundation* connects the other five components and contains model-based rapid application development tools, including a drag-and-drop mash-up builder for assembling dashboards and other applications. It also includes security and DevOps services as well as connection services for such things as tunneling servers. A subcomponent, ThingWorx Foundation Edge, comes with an edge microserver (server software for IoT edge devices) and a software development kit for PTC's AlwaysOn Protocol, which helps minimize devices' power and data demands.

2. *ThingWorx Utilities* help business users define, manage, monitor, and optimize their connected products as well as create and manage business processes related to the IoT devices. The resulting connectors are meant be reusable in new business processes and devices.

3. *ThingWorx Analytics* includes simulation and predictive analytics features to help users get value from the data collected from devices. The software can also detect anomalies and patterns in real-time data. An analytics server adds the ability to monitor devices for predicted outcomes (such as equipment failure) and optimize them by automatically detecting the reasons for certain outcomes.

4. *Vuforia* technology for augmented reality development.

5. *Kepware KepServerEX* is an IoT gateway and other network software for integrating industrial systems, including SCADA (supervisory control and data acquisition) and MES (manufacturing execution system) software.

In 2016, PTC (formerly Parametric Technology Corp.) announced support for public IoT device cloud services, including Amazon Web Services IoT and Microsoft Azure IoT Hub. Device cloud services handle integration with a variety of IoT devices so ThingWorx developers can concentrate on building applications that access the devices.

PTC ThingWorx has attracted significant third-party support. By mid-2016, the ThingWorx website listed just over 100 partners, notably Bosch, Cisco, Dell, Ericsson, Hitachi, Intel, Texas Instruments, and Verizon.

QiO

- *Platform:* Foresight
- *Launch:* June 2016
- *Industries:* energy and utilities, manufacturing, transportation and logistics
- *Use cases:* asset monitoring and predictive maintenance
- *Cloud:* private (Foresight cloud; available on-premise)

QiO consists of four applications:

1. *QiO Foresight Energy*® enables you to predict how energy fluctuations in your business will impact quality, production, and costs. Analyze data from your industrial equipment, Smart Meters, MES, and ERP systems to create a real-time energy efficiency index.

2. *QiO Foresight Maintenance*® significantly improves safety, lengthen asset life, reduces unplanned downtime and outages. Our AI-infused QiO Foresight Maintenance® application enables you to predict failures and recommend the best course of action for your team to prevent or mitigate them while minimizing downtime.

3. *QiO Foresight Performance*® digitally track compliance and collaborate on standards with sites and suppliers worldwide. QiO Foresight Performance® helps you quickly improve KPIs across your enterprise. Prebuilt templates with industry best practices for quality, safety, and lean make it easy to get started.

4. *QiO Foresight Production*® helps you deftly manage unexpected events that would otherwise lower productivity, efficiency, and quality. Our AI-infused QiO Foresight Production® application continuously monitors your shop-floor schedules and supply chain networks to predict resource challenges, such as material, parts, and labor, reducing costs and improving quality.

Although QiO's Foresight platform spans the full range of components for the industrial market, the company's strengths are its advanced analytics, and notably its digital twin for industrial assets. Its go-to-market partners include Rolls-Royce, Lloyd's Register, and BT.

SAP

- *Platform:* Leonardo
- *Launch:* January 2017
- *Industries:* energy and utilities, manufacturing, transportation and logistics
- *Use cases:* asset monitoring, predictive maintenance, related analytics
- *Cloud:* cloud and on-premise via SAP cloud platform

SAP Leonardo, see Figure 6.6, is considered a disruptive technology because of its transformative intelligence.

SAP Leonardo is the digital innovation system that coordinates the outer future-confronting advancements and capacities incorporated in the SAP Cloud Platform into one intellectual framework. With the help of this bimodal methodology, the SAP Leonardo advance services are conveyed on the SAP Cloud Platform confining you from a core platform from any risks or changes. With the help of SAP Leonardo, it is possible

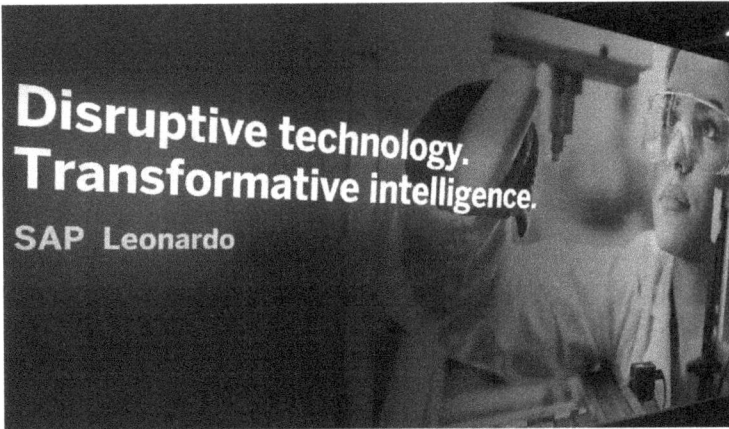

Figure 6.6 SAP Leonardo

Source: Computerworld

to open and power the upright cycle of innovation by combining SAP Leonardo into the expansiveness of the SAP portfolio.

The data and transactions that were just recorded in the framework will presently be utilized as the contributions for the arrangement of advancement that would give intelligent bits of knowledge and mechanize the business process. With SAP S/4HANA on the center, SAP Leonardo encourages the business to scale everywhere helping to computerize change by quickly embracing new business models and capacities and including future advances as they arise. Now, Licensing and Subscription ends up easier than any time in recent memory as it would be just for the technologies and skills that you would utilize: contribute in the administration than the product. SAP Leonardo is implanted using the SAP Leonardo's Innovative services.

SAP Leonardo combines all the recent technologies and services into a single intelligent system and includes the following functionality:

- *Machine learning:* SAP Leonardo includes ML capabilities to get the useful bits of knowledge powered by AI bits to take the informed business decisions.
- *Internet of Things:* SAP Leonardo also involves intelligently associated things, people, and processes and takes benefits of IIoT and Internet of Everything.

- *Big Data:* With the help of Big Data, it has the capability to store, manage, access, and interface with a broad scope of information from numerous sources in any shape such as structured or unstructured.
- *Analytics:* It can extract the keen data from a vast network of anonymous data. It can be utilized to discover answers to numerous business issues.
- *Blockchain:* This technology is used to accelerate transactions over secured stages and enhances transparency, trust, and perceptibility.
- *Design thinking:* Experts support in business ideation, quick prototyping, and business case development.

Software AG

- *Platform:* Cumulocity
- *Launch:* March 2017
- *Industries:* energy and utilities, manufacturing, transportation and logistics
- *Use cases:* asset monitoring, predictive maintenance
- *Cloud compatibility:* private, hybrid, public

Cumulocity—see Figure 6.7—gives you very fast visibility and control over your remote assets, be they houses, cars, machines, or any other assets that you need to manage.

Cumulocity provides

- *APIs* for extending the existing functionality or interfacing Cumulocity with your other IT services such as ERP or CRM systems. Cumulocity can also host your HTML5 applications.
- *Certified software libraries* you can use to bring your remote assets into the cloud.
- *Device management,* data visualization, and remote control functionality through the web.
- *Rapid customization* of the aforementioned through real-time processing and Cumulocity applications.

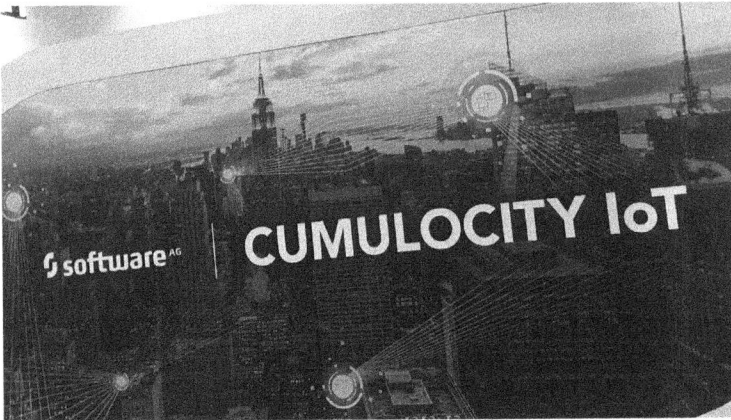

Figure 6.7 Software AG Cumulocity

Source: Enterprise IoT Insights

All this is provided through a cloud-based subscription service making the creation of IoT solutions with Cumulocity fundamentally different from bespoke development and RAD (rapid application development). You can start immediately with a large amount of existing functionality, and you can start for free. You do not need to worry about IT infrastructure (hosting, networking, security, storage, and backup) and IT management (all software is available to your users).

Cumulocity works with any network architecture, but is specifically designed to work out of the box with mobile networks. In the following sections, we will give a short overview of the different functional areas with references to more detailed descriptions.

Cumulocity has extensive customization options, for example:

- *Set up a graphical dashboard* with your most important KPIs.
- *Subscribe to plug-ins* that contribute new functionality to the Cumulocity application.
- Use real time to *implement real-time business rules*. For example, get an e-mail when critical events happen, or trigger automated actions on devices in that case.
- *Write alarm rules* to reprioritize or suppress alarms and to define your SLA parameters.

Chapter Takeaways

- The key components of an IIoT platform
- *Key factors to consider while choosing your IIoT platform*
- Overview of global IIoT platform vendors including platform name, launch date, target industries, use cases, and summary description

Management Questions for Your Business

- How do you create a short list of suitable IIoT platforms?
- How do you describe each IIoT platform on the short list, including benefits and risks, security and budgets for hardware, software, and personnel?
- How do you forecast tangible and intangible results or savings?
- What are the total forecasted costs or budgets and forecasted results or savings of each IIoT platform?
- What is the IIoT platform with the highest cash flow?

References and Additional Reading

Doumeingts, G., F.W. Jaekel, M. Wollschlaeger, and M. Zelm. 2018. *Enterprise Interoperability: Smart Services and Business Impact of Enterprise Interoperability.* London, UK and Wiley, Hoboken, NJ: ISTE Ltd.

Sahoo, P. 2019. *Optimizing Current Strategies and Applications in Industrial Engineering,* IGI Global, Herschey, P.A.

http://dzone.com/

http://engineering.com/

http://enterpriseiotinsights.com/

http://iotworldtoday.com/

https://ittechnologynews24.com/

http://simpleiot.eu/

http://smartfactoryvn.com/

CHAPTER 7

Opportunities, Challenges, and Trends

Where to get started to discover where AI might be a good fit? Here are five important questions you should be asking to help results-oriented AI opportunities in your organization.

- *What business outcome do we want to achieve?* Let business needs and goals dictate sensible applications of AI. Always align your AI initiatives with your overall business strategies. It makes no sense to invest in an area that does not have a clear impact on business goals. If you ignore this, you will never make it to production and be stuck in proof-of-concept purgatory.
- *Where are we most inefficient?* Identify which of your processes have measurable inefficiencies. A mostly universal example would be to look for critical processes or tasks in your business that rely heavily (or entirely) on manual data entry.
- *Where can we make better decisions?* One of the fundamental opportunities for AI or AI-augmented solutions lies in any process or area where your organization can improve its decision making. In particular, where would your organization benefit from moving to a more data-driven model?
- *Where do we have a lot of relevant data?* AI depends upon the information you feed it. While that could ultimately come from all manner of sources, the early phases of identifying promising AI opportunities will likely be better served by considering areas in which you have robust, reliable, and accessible data.

- *Will this actually solve our problem?* Too few companies ask
  this question during their AI exploration. It is common to
  identify business problems for which there is a relevant AI
  project, but where the project will not solve the problem. This
  is common in AI projects aimed at driving better business
  efficiency.

Cyber-security breaches are becoming more intense. A host of new threats involving phishing, crypto jacking, IoT attacks, malware, SQL injection, and a lot more are a huge concern for anyone in the online world. An option available to boost cyber-security is the Blockchain technology.

Blockchain uses a combination of public and private keys to store and send virtual assets. The public key creates the address of where the assets are stored in the public ledger. The private key is used to sign each transaction a user sends out and prove that the user requesting the transaction does in fact have ownership of the assets. Anyone can have access to the public key, but as long as the private key remains a secret, the assets are safe. But if a private key is lost or stolen, the assets associated with it are gone forever. Herein lies the fundamental shortfall that undermines the security of Blockchain solutions—protecting private keys.

It is apparent that the security challenges, specifically the vulnerability of private keys, must be addressed before the full potential of Blockchain technology can be realized. Multisignature improves security by introducing additional distributed keys for recovery and authentication. Yet, this still relies on the use of original keys. To meet this critical market gap, multisignature can be combined with proven tokenization technology. Tokenization is a process that replaces sensitive credentials—such as private keys for Blockchain—with a nonsensitive equivalent token that is unique to each transaction. In doing so, tokenization mitigates fraud risk and protects the underlying value of credentials. This adds a layer of frictionless security that complements the immutability of the Blockchain.

For Blockchain technology to be truly transformative, a secure foundation of trust and transparency is needed—starting with a new approach to security. Tokenization technology is an immediately available solution to provide this foundation.

A specific area where the convergence of Blockchain, IoT, and AI will play a prominent role is in smart manufacturing. See Figure 7.1.

Figure 7.1 Smart manufacturing and IoT

Source: Gemalto

Opportunities Enabled by AI

Business innovation and the opportunities they create are how enterprises distinguish themselves from one another. It is how they do things better, how they create value, and ultimately, how they pass that value over to the customer. Business innovation is a continuous effort that is empowered by technologies and methodologies that are available at any given moment. Today, that technology is AI.

Many of you are likely familiar with the AI enablers to follow; some have worked with them first hand. Others are likely familiar with the applications, but may not have known that AI is playing an important role in the background. Regardless, my point is to inspire you to think differently about AI and how it can impact your business. Like many new technologies, the full potential of AI is being realized slowly, and it only takes someone exploring the possibilities around them to discover something new.

Enablers of Innovation

- *Big Data:* Here is the thing about Big Data—it's massive. It has to be in order to reveal patterns and associations, and predict trends accurately. However, while humans do have the capacity to discover patterns and predict trends, it is an impossibility at the scale in which modern enterprise demands. For AI, it is impressively suited to glean through large data sets in order to quickly and most of all accurately derive actionable insights.

- *Deep learning:* In AI, the word that stands out most is intelligence, which is also the ability to learn. Deep learning does just that, by utilizing AI neural networks to act as a human brain would, analyzing and learning all without the aid of a computer programmer. This ability to "think" on its own is a driving force behind such innovations as autonomous vehicles, which are great, as keeping a computer programmer in the trunk of your car isn't a feasible option.

- *Reinforcement learning (RL):* RL is an important type of machine learning where "machines" learn how to behave in an environment by performing actions and seeing the results, not unlike students in a classroom. This behavior can be learnt based on a reward mechanism, or keep on adapting as time goes by. RL algorithms can converge to establish an ideal behavior baseline, especially for robotics, autonomous driving, and process control.

- *Applications and Opportunities (see Figure 7.2)*

- *Autonomous vehicles:* The automobile market is enormous; however, it's still a limited market. That is because while anybody can buy a car, not everyone can drive one. That is, they couldn't before AI came along. People who are blind or suffer from certain physical limitations will soon have the ability to go anywhere thanks to this new technology. The use of these self-driving cars in logistics is an innovative application and is already being tested with prodigious results.

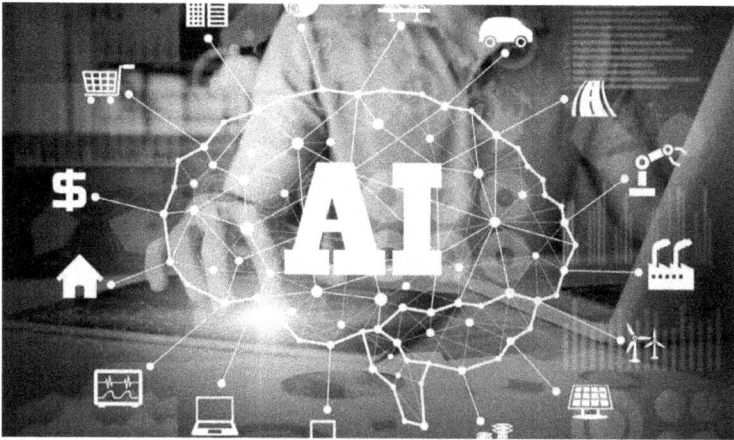

Figure 7.2 Opportunities enabled by AI

Source: Business Opportunities

- *Behavior prediction:* Anyone in business knows that the customer is the most important actor, which is why perhaps so much time is spent trying to guess what they'll want next. Thanks to AI these predictions have gone from guesswork to science. AI and its ability to analyze massive data sets give you the ability to learn more about their customers, such as their shopping habits, preferences, and even churn rate.
- *Chatbots:* Thanks to AI, chatbots have grown more sophisticated and are almost indistinguishable from humans. In fact, chatbots are often a better alternative than using traditional CSR. Instant response to inquiries, reduced service time, fewer errors, increased customer engagement, the ability to handle simple transactions, and proactive customer interactions are all within the grasp of these bots.
- *Content creation:* Content isn't just a way for you to get your message to the customer, it's a way to provide that customer with value. AI is increasing the efficiency in how we do that by allowing us to deliver personalized content to the user and by helping inform our strategy through insightful data

analysis. Creation aside, AI already does aid in the distribution of content, allowing for more efficient and documented campaigns.

- *Customer relationship management:* CRM systems were in and of themselves a considerable business innovation, one that continues to yield results for sales teams. Given the success rates of such implementations, AI is poised to do what sales teams and CRM alone can't. From transcribing and analyzing calls to qualifying, engaging, nurturing, and following up with leads via e-mail, AI is positioned to do more for the customers you serve.

- *Customer service:* Whether they have made a purchase or not, and regardless of how far along in the buyer's journey, any good enterprise needs to ensure that the customer's demands are met. However, given the multitude of touchpoints on that journey, this can be difficult. For AI, however, it can act as a "gatekeeper" throughout the experience handling simple questions.

- *Decision making:* When asked the key to their success, it isn't uncommon to hear powerful men and women give credit to "trusting their gut." And while this may be your best option in certain situations, the modern business landscape is unlikely to be one of them. AI has given you the ability to weigh the variables, judge potential outcomes, and make the best decision based on the relevant data.

- *Digital marketing:* Marketing is usually only effective when the right message gets to the right audience on the right channel. Thanks to AI targeted messaging across channels is becoming easier and more effective than ever. This will help ensure that marketing dollars are spent in more effective ways and can also help to tailor messages that are appropriate for whatever stage of the buyer journey the customer finds themselves.

- *HR and recruitment:* HR and recruitment are by nature a very people-oriented vertical. However, that should be no indication that AI integration isn't applicable. HR is filled with numerous rule-based tasks that could be done much better by AI. Let's take on-boarding, for example. It would take an HR associate 2.5 hours to complete from hiring decision to sending the welcome e-mail, while an AI-fueled substitute could accomplish the same in just 8 minutes.

- *Intrusion detection:* While technology has enabled us to do more, it has also caused us to be more conscious and aware, especially when we are potentially vulnerable to digital intrusion. Current defense against cyber-attacks are generally responsive; however, with AI's help, this can be switched to proactive. With AI, you can set a baseline of normal activity on your network and more accurately recognize potential threats if they deviate from typical behavior.

- *Logistics and delivery:* A product is only of value if it reaches the hands of the customer, and this is why logistics and delivery is so crucial to business success. Integrating AI in your supply chain can unify your data, analyzing and providing insights across the organization as well as streamline the customs brokerage process. However, in predictive analytics we see the most significant value, through demand prediction, route optimization, and network management.

- *Manufacturing:* Today, AI and its ability to reason, theorize, and forecast is what has the manufacturing world excited. From improving predictive maintenance, reducing supply chain forecasting errors, and reducing energy costs through demand forecast, the benefits of AI in manufacturing directly impact the bottom line. Few moments in history are marked by the presence of a technology that is so adaptable, has such widespread potential, and can impact as many verticals across as many industries, as AI.

- *Payment services:* Life is filled with some certainties that go beyond death and taxes. For example, like everyone else, you regularly need milk, fruit, toilet paper, and a variety of other "staples." AI, as your own personal "butler," can make those authorized payments and arrange for shipping to your home when your supply is getting low. Anyone with kids will quickly see the value of always having the essentials on hand.

- *Robotic process automation (RPA):* While we hope everyone loves what they do for a living, the reality is that even the best "dream jobs" have their periods of boring and monotonous work. In fact, some jobs seem to be exclusively filled with such processes. But it doesn't have to be. AI-fueled RPA currently replicates basic rule-based tasks much faster, accurately, and cost-effectively than humans.

- *Translation:* Whether you are a business traveler or looking to branch out into new international markets, one of the most significant barriers to not only business but people is language. Thanks to AI, more and more companies are expanding into new markets, no longer restricted by language. And while technology has made the world a smaller place, I believe it is AI that will help empower true universal communication.

Opportunities Enabled by Blockchain of Things

The Blockchain of Things is changing the world as we speak. It's not only dominating the industrial landscape but also our day-to-day lives as we know it. In reality, the Blockchain of Things solely depends on the connectivity of the world. The Blockchain of Things technologies are overly hyped with very few knowledge of what they do.

Not to mention the enormous amount of data the Blockchain of Things can deal with. Thus, it's crucial that enterprises keep on exploring the Blockchain of Things for the betterment of the future. Even though IoT did have some major setbacks mainly in security, with a Blockchain of Things network, those setbacks will be long gone. The Blockchain of Things also enables you to elevate your business value as you can see in Figure 7.3.

Here are a few opportunities that may inspire you to improve your business:

Figure 7.3 Blockchain of Things to elevate your business value

Source: ValueCoders

- *Better automation Process*: The use of automation comes with its fair share of risks. But using only a single autonomous system to manage thousands of data isn't a great option. A single change in the code could bring down the whole industry. Or if a hacker gets into the system and changes just one simple number, it can affect the data the system is maintaining. So, you would need the Blockchain of Things to manage the automation process so that no one can get access to it. If anyone highjacks the results, the process would normally break down. As the Blockchain of Things platform is immutable, it would prevent anyone from changing the results. Thus, the Blockchain of Things will prevent any risky automation processes for good.
- *Better compliances*: There are so many scenarios involving processes where you need to know if they are properly complied with. Additionally, this goes mainly for processes involving multiple parties. Anyhow you can get a better compliance experience with the help of smart contracts in the Blockchain of Things system. The Blockchain of Things use cases can foresee whether particular compliance is being met or not. Furthermore, the Blockchain of Things system can also stop

any further compliances if previous compliances aren't met properly.

- *Better quality control in IoT manufacturing*: The manufacturing stage is quite crucial for IoT devices. In reality, there's no quality control whatsoever. The security issues of these devices keep on piling up. Moreover, instead of focusing on security, they mainly focus on design esthetics. But with the help of the Blockchain of Things use cases, the scenario will change entirely. With the Blockchain of Things system, the companies can manage the quality of every single device they produce, not only for the physical security but in the software security as well. The enormous amount of devices can become quite overwhelming to perfect. But with the help of the Blockchain of Things, they can easily pull it off.

- *Collaborative environment for shared economy*: The sharing economy is one of the rising industries at present. Furthermore, it's an economy where peer-to-peer sharing of services, goods, or any other kind of resources happen. Needless to say, almost all the shared economy industry heavily depends on the credibility of the IoT devices. In this case, the Blockchain of Things is the perfect catch. With the help of the Blockchain of Things, you can even create a collaborative environment as well. So, I have to say the Blockchain of Things makes the perfect pair for this industry as well.

- *Data anonymity for extra privacy*: IoT is not only for enterprise users but also for our daily lives. In reality, almost everything of a smart home is equipped with this technology. However, with this much intimate exposure to these devices, our privacies are in huge jeopardy. In many cases, these devices can pass our private information to the outside world. Thus, we are no longer in full control of our own sensitive information. Blockchain of Things use cases can help out here as well.

- *Encryption for multifactor authorization*: Do you know how our passwords aren't enough to offer full security anymore? With the default password choices from the manufacturer, it became relatively easy for any hacker just to guess it and get access. In reality, many don't use multifactor passwords or authorization methods. So, it becomes way more prone to hacks. With the Blockchain of Things network, you will get multifactor authorizations that may include biometric identities as well. All the multifactor authorization keys would also be encrypted and stored in the Blockchain of Things system to offer full security.

- *End-to-end visibility*: A full transparent network is a trusted network. In reality, the issue with our typical centralized servers is the lack of full transparency. Thus, many are skeptical of whether they can trust the system or not. Furthermore, it's more common within the enterprises too. With the help of Blockchain of Things use cases, now no one would face this dilemma. The Blockchain of Things is capable of offering full-time end-to-end visibility.

- *Firewall against distributed denial of service (DDoS) attacks*: Remember how the DDoS attack can cripple an enterprise network? Many enterprises fall prey to these abusive attacks that take down their whole network space within a few minutes. The IoT devices are much more vulnerable and prone to DDoS attacks. The hackers can easily find out vulnerable IoT devices in a network and attack them, causing the whole network to crash down. But with the help of Blockchain of Things use cases, all of the DDoS attacks can be solved.

- *High data security*: According to a recent survey, over 81 percent of enterprises, government, and corporations believe that an IoT disaster will affect them in the upcoming two years. However, only 28 percent of them are doing anything about it. We'll eventually have no means of protecting ourselves from the outer threats. Thus, the Blockchain of Things use cases can really come in handy here. With Blockchain of Things use cases, the enterprise will get a full proof secured network that can offer the facilities no third-party provider can offer.

- *Identity for IoT devices*: There's another major issue in the IoT industry, and it's the lack of identity for the IoT devices. Typically there's no way to check the authenticity of the device. Furthermore, simple company status or when it was created isn't even available for verification. Moreover, where the IoT device is updating the software or whether it has an issuer signature or not is something that users should know. But with the help of Blockchain of Things use cases, now they can know for sure.

- *More access control*: All of the connected devices can highly benefit from the Blockchain of Things system. Furthermore, the Blockchain of Things use cases can fully offer access control for both virtual and physical resources. Moreover, the system is also capable of storing the record of who accesses what kind of resources all the time. With the help of Blockchain of Things use cases, you can even specify individuals and their level of access.

- *Real-time tracking*: A major component of IoT is the sensors and RFID tags. With these, anyone can track objects to ensure their full authenticity. In reality, due to the lack of proper tracking system, many manufacturers face issues in trade. Not only trade but also the supply chain is in dire need of real-time tracking. In reality, the IoT devices are capable of handling all the tracking, but they need risk management as well. So, with the help of Blockchain of Things use cases, any company can now track their goods without any issues.

- *Stronger cloud management*: Cloud is a huge part of the IoT architecture. Mainly the devices are always working collecting information, processing it, sending it back and forth. Sometimes some IoT devices can send the information to the cloud without ever encrypting it. As a result, hackers can easily get access to it and use it to their own benefit. In reality, even the cloud isn't fully capable of handling all the security issues. As there are many networks on the same cloud, sometimes data leaks occur. But with the Blockchain of Things solution, you can easily protect the cloud more efficiently. Thus, with the Blockchain of Things, the cloud would be safer than ever.

- *Stronger data validation process*: The popularity and demand for Big Data is rising tremendously on the marketplaces. In reality, it's quite evident that by the year 2023, it will become a $100+ billion industry. But why is that? Well, data is becoming a huge part of our lives and is the most desired product of all time. Moreover, we get so many data from all the IoT devices, computers, and so on. However, we don't have any good technology to really verify whether the data is valid or not. With Blockchain of Things system on the rise, it would be finally possible.

Cyber-Security Threats

In October 2016, a hacker found a vulnerability on a specific model of security cameras. Nearly 300,000 IoT video recorders started to attack multiple social network websites and brought down Twitter and other high-profile platforms, for almost two hours.

This attack is just an example of what can happen to IoT devices with poor security.

It is not only video cameras, but anything with an Internet connection, from a refrigerator, smart locks, thermostats, light bulbs, vehicles, and even smart toys. Using them always poses IoT security challenges and risks to overcome.

IoT Security Challenges

Now, it is not only us with our computers, but there are also "things" that interact with the Internet without our intervention. These "things" are continually communicating with the Internet, a fridge sending an update of the food inside or our vehicle transmitting messages to the mechanic to inform its oil levels.

IoT is wonderful in many ways. But unfortunately, technology has not matured yet, and it is not entirely safe. The entire IoT environment, from manufacturers to users, still has many security challenges of IoT to overcome, such as:

- Manufacturing standards
- Update management
- Physical hardening
- Users knowledge and awareness

Top IoT Security Risks

Returning to what happened in 2016, the lack of compliance on the part of IoT manufacturers led to weak and unprotected passwords in some IoT video cameras, which, in turn, led to one of the most damaging botnet attacks, the Mirai malware. To save your assets from being attacked, you really need to secure them, like you can see in Figure 7.4.

There are many IoT security threats, but I'm highlighting the most important ones:

Figure 7.4 Cyber-security threats

Source: Enterprise Talks

- *Botnet attacks*: A single IoT device infected with malware does not pose any real threat. It's a collection of them that can bring down anything. To perform a botnet attack, a hacker creates an army of bots by infecting them with malware and directs them to send thousands of requests per second to bring down the target. IoT security became serious after the Mirai bot attack in 2016. Multiple DDoS attacks using hundreds of thousands of IP cameras and home routers were infected. IoT devices are highly vulnerable to malware attacks and are quickly turned into infected zombies and used as weapons to send incredibly vast amounts of traffic.

- *Cryptomining with IoT bots*: Mining cryptocurrency demands colossal CPU resources, and another IoT security issue has emerged due to this precondition—cryptomining with IoT bots. This type of attack involves infected botnets aimed at IoT devices, with the goal not to create damage, but mine cryptocurrency. The open-source cryptocurrency Monero is one of the first ones to be mined using infected IoT devices, such as video cameras. Although a video camera does not have powerful resources to mine cryptocurrency, an army of them does. IoT botnet miners pose a great threat to the crypto market, as they have the potential to flood and disrupt the entire market in a single attack.

- *Data integrity risks of IoT security in health care*: With IoT, data is always on the move. It is being transmitted, stored, and processed. Most IoT devices extract and collect information from the external environment. But sometimes these devices send the collected data to the cloud without any encryption. As a result, a hacker can gain access to a medical IoT device, gaining control over it and being able to alter the data it collects. A controlled medical IoT device can be used to send false signals, which in turn can make health practitioners take actions that may damage the health of their patients. There are risks of IoT security in health care devices like pacemakers or the ones making the insulin shots.

- *Hijacking your IoT devices*: Ransomware, one of the nastiest malware types, doesn't destroy your sensitive files—it blocks access to them by way of encryption. The hacker who infected the device will then demand a ransom fee for the decryption key unlocking the files. The cases of IoT devices infected with ransomware are rare, but becoming a trend. Wearables, health care gadgets, and other smart devices might be at risk in the future. Here's good news and bad news. While this malware might not have valuable data to lock down since IoT information is stored in the cloud, it can lock down the device's functionality. Imagine your vehicle will not start unless you pay a ransom fee—or your house is locked down.

- *Industrial espionage and eavesdropping*: If hackers take over surveillance in a location by infecting IoT devices, spying might not be the only option. They can also perform such attacks to demand ransom money. Spying and intruding through IoT devices is a real problem, as a lot of different sensitive data may be compromised. On an industrial level, a company's Big Data can be collected by hackers to expose sensitive business information. Some countries are starting to ban specific IoT devices with security problems. For example, the interactive IoT doll with a Bluetooth pin was labeled as an espionage device and was banned in Germany.

- *IoT security problems in device update management*: Another source of IoT security risks is insecure software or firmware. Although a manufacturer can sell a device with the latest software update, it is almost inevitable that new vulnerabilities will come out. Updates are critical for maintaining security on IoT devices. Some IoT devices continue being used without the necessary updates. Another risk is that during an update, a device will send its backup out to the cloud and will suffer a short downtime. If the connection is unencrypted and the update files are unprotected, a hacker could steal sensitive information.

- *Lack of compliance of IoT manufacturers*: New IoT devices come out almost daily, all with undiscovered vulnerabilities.

The primary source of most IoT security issues is that manufacturers do not spend enough time and resources on security. The following are some security risks in IoT devices from manufacturers:

- Weak, guessable, or hard-coded passwords
- Hardware issues
- Lack of a secure update mechanism
- Old and unpatched embedded operating systems and software
- Insecure data transfer and storage
- *Lack of physical hardening*: The lack of physical hardening can also cause IoT security issues. Although some IoT devices should be able to operate autonomously, they need to be physically secured from outer threats. Sometimes, these devices can be located in remote locations for long stretches of time. Building secure sensors and transmitters in the already low-cost devices is a challenging task for manufacturers. Users are also responsible for keeping IoT devices physically secured. A smart motion sensor or a video camera that sits outside a house could be tampered with if not properly protected.
- *Lack of user knowledge and awareness*: IoT is a new technology, and people still do not know much about it. While most of the risks of IoT security issues are still on the manufacturing side, users and business processes can create bigger threats. One of the biggest IoT security risks and challenges is the user's ignorance and lack of awareness of the IoT functionality. A type of IoT security risk that is often overlooked is social engineering attacks. Instead of targeting devices, a hacker targets a human, using the IoT. Social engineering was used in the 2010 Stuxnet attack against a nuclear facility in Iran.
- *Rogue IoT devices*: Considering the rapid growth of the number of IoT devices, predicted by Ericsson to reach 18 billion by 2022, the problem with this number of devices arises not only in enterprises, but also in home networks. One of the most significant IoT security risks is *that rogue devices or*

counterfeit malicious IoT devices are beginning to be installed in secured networks without authorization. A rogue device replaces an original one or integrates as a member of a group to collect or alter sensitive information. These can be turned into a rogue AP (Access Point), thermostat, or video camera and intercept incoming data communications unknown to users. Other variations of rogue devices may also emerge in the future.

Cyber War Threats

Cyber warfare refers to the use of technology to launch attacks on nations, governments, and citizens, causing comparable harm to actual warfare using weaponry.

To date, there hasn't been an outright "cyber war" with declared antagonists; however, there are a number of incidents that have caused serious disruption to countries' infrastructure that are suspected of being carried out by another state. In the first quarter of 2019 there have been 29 cyber warfare attacks at the U.S. national level as described in Figure 7.5.

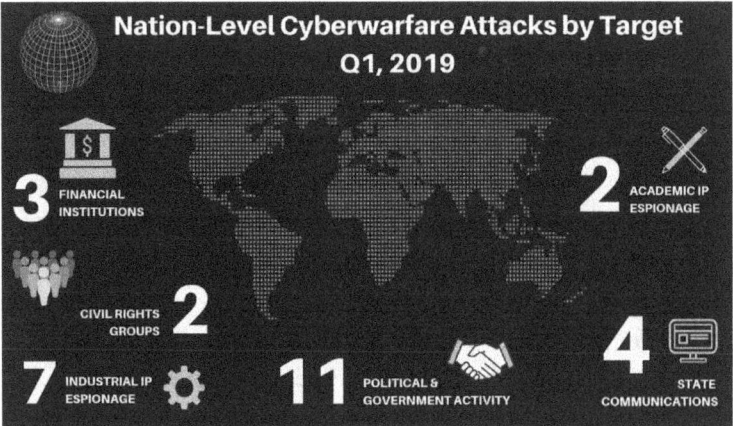

Figure 7.5 Cyber warfare attacks by target

Source: CPO Magazine

Cyber warfare according to the *Oxford English Dictionary* is "The use of computer technology to disrupt the activities of a state or organization, especially the deliberate attacking of information systems for strategic or military purposes."

The problem with cyber warfare is that it's very hard to work out who launched the attack in the first place. In many cases, nobody will claim responsibility for the attacks and while it may be possible to speculate based on the geopolitical situation, there will never be a solid answer, particularly as states will find it easier to cover their tracks than individuals. In others, hacking collectives may quickly take responsibility, but while it's often strongly suspected these are "state-sponsored" attackers, the strength of direct links with an antagonistic state can be hard to prove.

Who's Under Cyber Warfare Attack?

The answer, if you go by the dictionary definition, is an unequivocal yes. Along with most western countries, there are concerted cyber-attacks pretty much daily against government organizations and enterprises alike. But are we engaged in a cyber war? Not according to the "clear and unambiguous" attribution requirement.

We know that Russia and China are developing cyber weapons to use in any future cyber conflict, and the United States, France, and Israel are just as active as nation states leading the way in this endeavor. But that doesn't mean we can say any of these countries are using them, although we know they have the capability and have done so in the past. Stuxnet, for example, was a joint venture between Israel and the United States to destroy Iran's nuclear program capability.

What Weapons Are Used in Cyber War?

Primarily, the weapons are not dissimilar to those we see being used in criminal attacks all the time. Here botnets are ready to launch DDoS attacks that can cause widespread disruption to critical services or act as resource-diverting smokescreen for other activity on the network—or both. Social engineering and spear phishing techniques are also used to introduce an attacker into the system of an adversary. The insider threat is a very real weapon in the cyber warfare armory, with a mole able to introduce a threat directly to the network.

Stuxnet, discovered in 2010, is a great example of how multiple layers of attack can be successfully used. Someone working within the Iranian nuclear power program knowingly or unknowingly physically inserted a USB stick infected with the Stuxnet worm into a system.

The malware, which used multiple zero-day exploits, searched for specific software controlling centrifuges, and once located reprogrammed them to spin dangerously fast then slow, undetectably, for a period of several months. Eventually, the centrifuges broke, and more than 1,000 machines were effectively destroyed.

Although nobody has ever claimed responsibility for the attack, it's widely believed this cyber weapon was created as a joint effort by the Israeli and U.S. military. Indeed, neither country has ever denied it and it's alleged that Stuxnet was played as part of a show reel at the retirement party of the head of the Israeli Defense Force (IDF).

Other Examples of Cyber War Threats

While Stuxnet is one of the best examples of cyber warfare in action, there are other significant events that can be attributed to state-level attacks.

One recent example comes from Russia, a country that has been accused of many and various state-level cyber-attacks. Russia is accused of mounting multiple cyber-attacks against Ukraine, including the BlackEnergy attack that cut the power to 700,000 homes in the country in 2015 and the NotPetya malware, which masqueraded as ransomware but was in reality designed purely to destroy the systems it infected.

North Korea, which has been generating headlines over its nuclear posturing and turbulent diplomatic relationship with the United States, has also been active in cyberspace. According to researchers, the North Korean state has been linked to the prolific and dangerous hacking organization codenamed HIDDEN COBRA, also known as the Lazarus Group. Both the Sony hack of 2014 and the hack of a Bangladeshi bank in 2016 were pinned on these hackers.

False Flags

The only cyber weapon that is perhaps even more dangerous and disruptive than the zero-day is the false flag. We know that, for example, the attack by the so-called "Cyber Caliphate," claiming to be affiliated to ISIS, on a U.S. military database was a false flag operation by the Russian state-sponsored hacking group APT 28. Why does this matter? Because the United States retaliated with kinetic attacks on cyber communication channels and drone strikes against human targets in Syria.

AI to Combat Terrorism and Crime

Narco-terrorism has had several meanings since its coining in 1983. It once denoted violence used by drug traffickers to influence governments or prevent government efforts to stop the drug trade. In the last several years, narco-terrorism has been used to indicate situations in which terrorist groups use drug trafficking to fund their other operations.

The several decades long "war on drugs" and the more recent "war on terror" have found common ground in countering the threat of narco-terrorism, thus combining two threats that have traditionally been treated separately. The concept of narco-terrorism originates from an understanding that the two phenomena of narcotics trafficking and terrorism are interconnected and subsequently that a coordination of antidrug and antiterror policy can be used, and is necessary, to effectively deal with both threats. That a link exists between the narcotics trade and terrorist organizations, as implied in the term narco-terrorism, has been known to exist for decades, yet the international focus on terrorism since September 11, 2001, has also increased the attention given to the phenomenon of narco-terrorism. Although traditionally a concept connected with Latin America, in contemporary policy, narco-terrorism is increasingly linked to the regions of Central and Southeast Asia.

Counter-Narcotics and -Terrorism Policy

The traditional separation of narcotics and terrorism countermeasures and agencies has gradually faded since 9/11. The urge for increased cooperation between law enforcement and intelligence agencies is advocated on a national, regional, and international level. This can easily be seen when reviewing the many conferences, meetings, and conventions signed on drug- and terrorism-associated security issues. Conventions contain clauses on the necessity for cooperation on combating narcotics and terror in concert, arguing that since both networks are interlinked in practice, they are inseparable in policy considerations. Focusing on the link between narcotics and terrorism, the law enforcement efforts and intelligence gathering agencies began a more developed framework for cooperation, and the war on drugs and the war on terror became interlinked:

- *Intelligence gathering*: Combining the two wars is based on the similarities of the threats, and the tools used to combat drug trafficking and terrorism are identical. Much of the counter-narcotics and counter-terrorism measures are dependent on intelligence gathering to receive information on networks, individuals, shipments, money laundering systems, and plans of forthcoming activities or attacks.
- *Law enforcement*: The narco-terrorism concept has also led to the merger of legal acts. The Vital Interdiction of Criminal Terrorist Organizations (VICTORY), a bill proposed in 2003, is being discussed in the United States. The act is intended to extend the powers of the Justice Department's mandate according to the Providing Appropriate Tools Required to Intercept and Obstruct Terrorism (PATRIOT) Act of 2001. This proposed act would give the department the right to investigate drug dealers, terrorists, and narco-terrorists.
- *Security analysis*: The focus in policymaking on the linkages between drug criminals and terrorist serves an important function to enhance effectiveness of countermeasures taken in these areas. Moreover, the recognized connection between these networks also provides for a more holistic perspective of security analysis, enabling analysts to incorporate several factors relevant for a complete security analysis of organized crime and organized nonstate violence.

So How to Combat Narco-Terrorism?

Advancements in AI and robotics have resulted in what was once science fiction or obscure academic research becoming increasingly integral to the very functioning of modern society. The massive growth in computational power and increasing abundance of data that characterized the "Digital Revolution" and the subsequent "Information Age" have been at the core of this, vastly improving capabilities and broadening the range of real-world applications for AI and robotics. The transformative potential of these technologies is already being leveraged by health care, agriculture, automotive, manufacturing, energy, financial, communications, entertainment, retail, and many more sectors, to enhance efficiency, improve powers of prediction, optimize resource allocation, reduce costs, create new revenue opportunities, and contribute to the fulfillment of the 2030 Agenda for Sustainable Development.

From a narco-terrorism perspective, AI and robotics also have enormous potential; see Figure 7.6.

These technologies can support in:

- Identification of persons of interest
- Stolen vehicles or suspicious sounds and behavior
- Predicting trends in criminality and support law enforcement to optimize resources

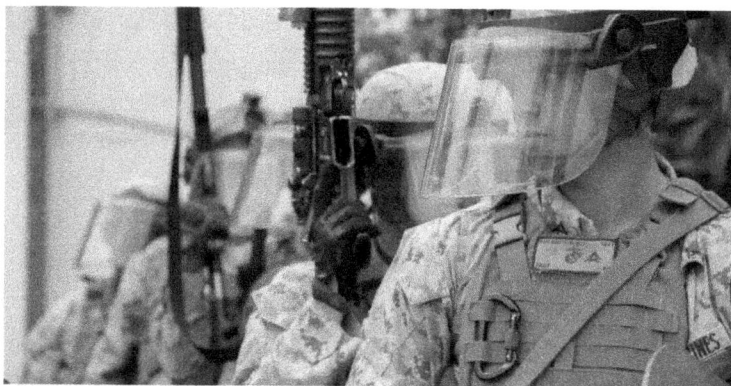

Figure 7.6 AI usage in counter-terrorism

Source: AI Tech Reporter

- Interpreting irregularities in financial transactions that might indicate fraud, corruption, or financing of terrorism
- Identifying and reporting child sexual abuse material
- Flagging and responding to terrorist use of the Internet
  At the same time, in the hands of narco-terrorist organizations, AI and robotics can enable new digital, physical, and political threats. Although the integration of these technologies into narco-terrorism has yet to be substantially identified, preparedness for the emergence of new threats and crimes must be a priority as these technologies become more accessible and pervasive throughout society. For instance, the so-called deep fakes, or programmatically generated video, have already demonstrated to add a whole new dimension to the "fake news" problem.

Technology Alone Is Not Enough

Global policies and agencies are ill-equipped to respond to narco-terrorism and offer some policy recommendations for remedying that. Narco-terrorism is the merging of terrorism and drug trafficking. Terrorist organizations and narcotics traffickers each have much to offer the other. There's potential for symbiosis in the form of cooperation. Examination of the dynamics between terrorist organizations and drug traffickers, combined with an evaluation of the responses to narco-terrorism, makes it clear that current policy responses fail to recognize narco-terrorism as a unique challenge, and instead attempt to deal separately with terrorism and drug trafficking. This approach has the potential to actually worsen both situations. Countries need a narco-terrorism strategy and institutions in place to implement it.

The set of interactions between international narcotics traffickers and terrorists reflect the potential symbiosis between terrorists and drug traffickers. These interactions can become bonds that make narcotic traffickers and terrorists indistinguishable. Countries don't currently possess capabilities to combat narco-terrorism, leaving the hybrid threat unmatched. In order to effectively eliminate narco-terrorism, the national security strategy must add a counter narco-terrorism focus to its toolbox in addition to the current stove-piped counter-narcotics and counter-terrorism missions.

Privacy Threats

There is a long list of concerns when it comes to a major technology like AI. Its privacy concerns only make up a small proportion of those. Most people are rather more worried about whether the robots will rise up and *kill us all*. While that is the more attention-grabbing potential outcome, privacy concerns around AI technology are more immanent and definitely more realistic. In fact, AI is already creating multiple privacy issues today, much less at some point in the future! There are two sides to the issue of AI privacy. On the one side of the debate, there are those that believe that AI technologies mean the end of privacy as we know it. The other side of the argument is more positive. The idea is that AI could actually actively protect our privacy.

The AI privacy issues that worry people today are largely based on how AI can be used to go through the mountains of data generated by Internet users and then create *algorithms* that can deduce things about you from very little information. What this means is that if those who have access to those algorithms only know one or two things about you, they can "guess" other things about you with a high degree of accuracy. This really challenges the traditional notion of privacy invasion. Because you aren't being directly observed. Your private life is laid bare even if you've never leaked anything private about yourself. The other major form of AI privacy invasion comes from *deep learning* applications. For example, deep learning neural networks can identify faces in seconds. So if you are moving in a public space, just a single clear frame caught by a camera somewhere can help piece together your movements. Summarizing, see Figure 7.7 to become aware that privacy issues caused by AI need to be taken seriously and be solved as much as possible.

As we travel along this path where more and more of the world is connected and digital, things look grimmer for personal privacy. The march of IoT devices is probably the main vector through which AI will share the world with us. Essentially this is the trend where every appliance and machine becomes somewhat intelligent and network-connected. Smart

Figure 7.7 AI threat to privacy

Source: Tweak Library

cameras, self-driving cars, and home automation systems are primary examples. Being watched wherever you go, having every action you make be recorded, and then for that sum total of your digital being scrutinized by AI—that's a future that's almost upon us.

Here's the thing. People can use any new information technology to damage someone's privacy. The invention of tiny cameras and listening devices is one example. It's technically trivial these days to hide cameras and microphones in someone's private space and record everything that they do. The problem isn't that technology can do something in principle, it's that we allow or condone the use of technologies in particular ways. The state needs the permission of the judiciary to plant bugs in your home. We have checks and balances to mitigate technological privacy abuses. The biggest problem is that our laws are based on conceptions of privacy from what is essentially another world. Unfortunately, the wheels of legal reform turn very slowly.

There's now a new AI tool that reads through certain privacy policies for us, checks the details, and points out the main parts that need our attention and it's called Guard. Guard is a neural network application that reads privacy policies. Currently, it has only been created to read the policies of well-known popular services such as Tinder, Netflix, and LinkedIn. You can request Guard to add other services and companies to its list, but that's an on-going process. Guard not only reads the policies for you, but it breaks them down in an easy-to-read manner. For example, it shares information about past privacy scandals a company has gone through and the level and amount of threat you may be faced with if you agree to their terms and conditions.

Future Directions and Trends

AI, advanced data analysis, and blockchain will have a decisive impact on future business, market, and business organizational models. What awaits us is a hyper-technological and connected world, an immense intelligent platform with autonomous things, and an increasingly natural mix between the physical world and digital worlds—a scenario that cannot ignore privacy and ethics. Some of the future trends are in autonomous and intelligent things as you can see in Figure 7.8.

According to Gartner, the future directions and trends regarding the Blockchain of Intelligent Things are predicted in the following areas:

- *Advanced and augmented analytics*: It's a new way of analyzing data that exploits a specific area of AI, for example, *machine learning*, to transform not only the analysis process itself but also the way in which the resulting content from the

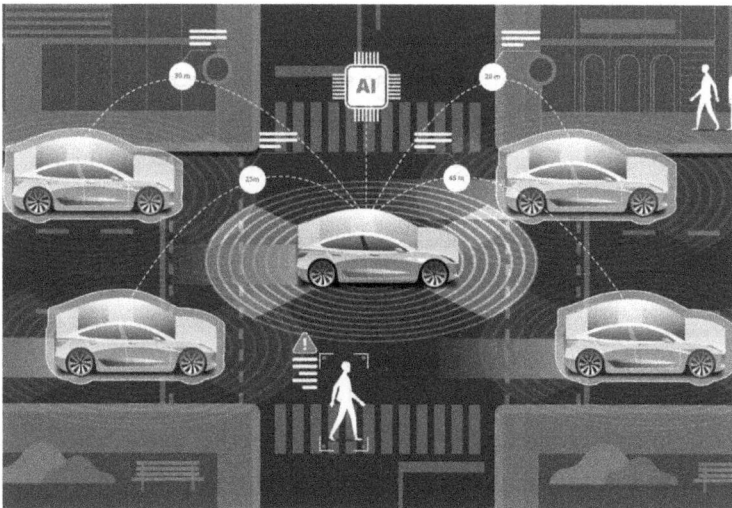

Figure 7.8 Autonomous intelligent vehicles

Source: Smart Cities World

analysis is consumed and shared. Gartner predicts that this type of analysis will produce *information and data that will be incorporated directly into the company,* in particular those related to customer services, finance, *HR, and marketing,* to optimize and speed up the decision-making processes. This ability will automate some processes, and Gartner also predicts that *by 2020 over 40 percent of data science activities will be automated,* resulting in increased productivity and wider use of data by all, not just "experts."

- *Autonomous and intelligent things:* In the next couple of years the objects will be exponentially based, on which there will be several AI systems such as *robots, autonomous vehicles, drones, appliances, and intelligent agents.* Gartner predicts that within a few years any type of service, application, and object based on the IoT will *integrate some form of AI to automate human processes,* decisions, and/or actions collaboratively human-to-machine and machine-to-machine. Pervasiveness is what will make the difference: it will no longer be just about having intelligent objects and systems in our world but seeing a *swarm of intelligent things that work together.* A possible scenario thanks to the Blockchain of Intelligent Things.

- *Blockchain technology:* The model of the "pure" blockchain, intended as an immutable and shared public record of transactions/actions, is still immature, little understood, and difficult to scale and expand globally. First of all, companies should start to become familiar with this technological architecture that promises radical changes in entire sectors, starting with finance. *Banks and financial services* companies are beginning to consider using blockchain to *simplify and optimize traditional banking operations* and to launch new cryptocurrencies that will be regulated or influenced by monetary policy. The blockchain also expands into other sectors where the cost of trade and contract closing times decreases and cash flow increases. *Blockchain will create 3.1 trillion dollars in terms of corporate value by 2030.*

- *Digital twins: By 2020, Gartner estimates there will be more than 20 billion connected sensors and terminations and potentially digital twins as copies of products and processes.* Already today, digital twins are models able to support and accelerate business processes, have independent analytical skills, and are able to do real-time analysis. These systems will evolve over time, improving their ability to collect and visualize data, apply the right rules, and respond effectively to business objectives to the point that you will soon hear about *DTO* (Digital Twin Organization), models that through data analysis will understand how an organization makes its business model operational, how it behaves on the market, how it distributes resources and responds to changes to *provide value to the customer.*

- *Intelligent spaces: An intelligent space* is a physical or digital environment in which human beings and technology interact in increasingly open and connected ecosystems: it's like saying that more elements including people, objects, services, processes, and so on, come together, move, and interact in an intelligent space to create a more interactive and automated experience. Just think of smart cities that represent the perfect example of *smart space,* but also digital workplace, *smart farms,* and *smart and connected factories* are concrete examples

- *Pervasiveness of AI*: AI will be more closely matched to the application development process to automate test phases. *By 2022, at least 40 percent of new projects will have codevelopers of AI in their team.* The main reason for this trend is to be found in a market that is rapidly shifting from an approach in which scientific data professionals must collaborate with application developers to create the most optimized solutions for AI to a model in which the professional developer can operate alone using models of advanced data analysis and AI predefined, even used as a service.

- *Privacy and ethics*: In the trends analysis, we also find the topic of *privacy and ethics,* a duty to face a future where data is the great protagonists of change. Gartner says that

Any discussion on privacy must be grounded in the broader topic of digital ethics and the trust of your customers, constituents and employees. While privacy and security are foundational components in building trust, trust is actually about more than just these components. Trust is the acceptance of the truth of a statement without evidence or investigation. Ultimately an organization's position on privacy must be driven by its broader position on ethics and trust.

Chapter Takeaways

- The BoIT provides many opportunities enabling Innovations, improving business value and to combat terrorism and crime
- The BoIT has to deal with challenges such as cyber-security threats, cyber war threats and privacy threats
- Future directions and trends are heading towards pervasiveness of AI and more autonomous and intelligent things

Management Questions for Your Business

- What business outcomes do we want to achieve?
- What processes are the most inefficient compared to the ones our competitors have?
- How would our organization benefit from moving to a more data-driven model to improve decision making?
- Where do we have a lot of reliable and accessible data?
- Will this actually solve our problems and challenges?
- What business opportunities are enabled by the Blockchain of Intelligent Things?
- How can we combat cyber war threats?
- How can we use AI to combat terrorism and crime?
- How can we protect our privacy with AI?
- What are the future directions and trends we will need regarding the Blockchain of Intelligent Things?

References and Additional Reading

Akhgar, B., and B. Brewster. 2017. *Combatting Cybercrime and Cyberterrorism: Challenges, Trends and Priorities.* Cham, Switzerland: Springer International Publishing.

Allen, P.R., and J.J. Bambara. 2020. *Blockchain, IoT, and Ai: Using the Power of Three to Develop Business, Technical, and Legal Solution.* New York, NY: McGraw-Hill Education.

Moore, M. 2017. *Cybersecurity Breaches and Issues Surrounding Online Threat Protection,* IGI Global, Herschey PA.

www.101blockchains.com/

www.coursehero.com/

www.diplomatie.gouv.fr/

www.dzone.com/

www.enterprisersproject.com/

www.intellectsoft.com/

www.itpro.co.uk/

www.medium.com/

www.paymentsjournal.com/

www.rambus.com/

www.tandofline.com/

www.technadu.com/

About the Author

Errol S. van Engelen is an author of management books located in Rotterdam, the Netherlands. He is also a 35+ year IT and business development veteran at technology and consulting companies. While working in a full-time career, he completed Marketing Management and Business Administration studies in the evening hours. He has been working independently since 2001 and has been focusing on digital transformation and emerging technologies.

Index

OTHER TITLES IN THE BIG DATA, BUSINESS ANALYTICS, AND SMART TECHNOLOGY COLLECTION

Mark Ferguson, University of South Carolina, Editor

- *Data-Driven Business Models for the Digital Economy* by Rado Kotorov
- *Highly Effective Marketing Analytics* by Mu Hu
- *Business Analytics, Volume II* by Amar Sahay
- *New World Technologies* by Errol S. van Engelen
- *Data Mining Models, Second Edition* by David L. Olson
- *Location Analytics for Business* by David Z. Beitz
- *Business Analytics, Volume I* by Amar Sahay
- *Introduction to Business Analytics* by Majid Nabavi
- *World Wide Data* by Linda Herkenhoff and John Fogli
- *Analytics Boot Camp* by Alfonso Asensio
- *Big Data War* by Patrick H. Park
- *Data Mining Models* by David Olson
- *Business Intelligence and Data Mining* by Anil Maheshwari

Announcing the Business Expert Press Digital Library

Concise e-books business students need for classroom and research

This book can also be purchased in an e-book collection by your library as

- a one-time purchase,
- that is owned forever,
- allows for simultaneous readers,
- has no restrictions on printing, and
- can be downloaded as PDFs from within the library community.

Our digital library collections are a great solution to beat the rising cost of textbooks. E-books can be loaded into their course management systems or onto students' e-book readers.
The **Business Expert Press** digital libraries are very affordable, with no obligation to buy in future years. For more information, please visit **www.businessexpertpress.com/librarians**. To set up a trial in the United States, please email **sales@businessexpertpress.com**.

www.ingramcontent.com/pod-product-compliance
Lightning Source LLC
Chambersburg PA
CBHW061219220326
41599CB00025B/4693